GCSE

Mathematics

Revision Course

Incorporating one-hour practice papers

J.J. McCarthy

BEd (Hons)

Higher
Tier

Levels 7 – 10

DP Publications Ltd
Aldine Place
London W12 8AW
1993

Acknowledgments

I would like to thank J.S. Simmons, Head of Mathematics, Bow School for Boys, for his useful suggestions during the preparation of this book, and SMILE Mathematics for permission to use diagrams from cards 1296 and 1352. I would also like to thank Jo Kemp and Liz Elwin at DP Publications for their help throughout.

A catalogue record for this book is available from the British Library

Copyright J.J. McCarthy © 1993

ISBN 185805 040 5

Typeset by DP Publications Ltd

Printed by The Guernsey Press Company Ltd, Braye Road, Vale, Guernsey, Channel Islands

Preface

Aim

The aim of this book is to provide a thorough **revision course**, enabling both practice and reinforcement of particular topics during your course, and cross-topic (examination-style) revision **immediately** prior to your examinations.

Need

The most effective way to revise for your GCSE mathematics paper is to practise on the sort of questions likely to be set, with the means of

a) knowing whether you tackle them **successfully**, and

b) **guidance** if you get stuck.

This book satisfies this need.

The GCSE and National Curriculum requirements

The GCSE tests you at the end of your National Curriculum Key Stage 4 course, and if you are entered for the Higher Tier of the GCSE, you are expected to have reached between Levels 7 and 10 of the National Curriculum at the time you sit the exam. The GCSE examination is divided into an end of course examination (representing 80% of the marks) and coursework (AT1, representing 20% of the marks) which your teacher will test you on **during** the course.

The National Curriculum in mathematics identifies five strands or topics in the course, known as Attainment Targets (ATs). These Attainment Targets are:

    ☐ *Using and applying mathematics*
      (usually known as 'coursework')   AT1

    ☐ *Number*   AT2

    ☐ *Algebra*   AT3

    ☐ *Shape and space*   AT4

    ☐ *Handling data*   AT5

This book provides all the practice required to meet the requirements of all the GCSE Mathematics Examination Board syllabuses at the Intermediate Tier *and* the National Curriculum at Key Stage 4.

Structure of the book

The book has three sections sections:

☐ **Section 1 – 15 one-hour practice Papers**

This section consists of 15 one-hour cross-topic practice papers that together will cover the whole of the GCSE syllabus and test Attainment Targets 2 to 5. These require written answers. The level of each question (ie Level 7, 8, 9 or 10) is indicated, and most of the questions have a 'helpline' reference to Section 2 where notes are available to assist you, eg AL7 is directing you to point 7 of the Algebra notes.

☐ **Section 2 – Revision notes and formulas**

This section contains a brief summary of the essential mathematical principles and formulas of the GCSE syllabus, organised by topic, with examples where necessary.

☐ **Section 3 – Answers to the one-hour practice papers**

In this section you will find all the answers to the questions in Section 1 and a marking scheme to enable you to record and interpret your marks for each paper.

How to use this book

The book is ideal for use prior to your GCSE examination when you have covered the topics in the course and need further practice and reinforcement. It can also be used at any stage of your GCSE course to practise and test particular topics you have covered or check whether you are confident at a particular level (ie Level 7, 8 ,9 or 10). If you want to work on a particular topic, say Algebra, use the **Question analysis by topic** grid on page vii to identify which questions on the papers deal with Algebra, and work through these, referring to the Section 2 information as and when you need it. If you want to check that you have reached a certain level, say 8, across the whole syllabus, work through the papers answering only those questions up to and including Level 8 (indicated next to the question and in the grid on page vii).

Each paper is intended to take you one hour to complete, but do take longer over each one if you wish, particularly in the early stages of revision. In your final revision, when you are doing each paper in one hour, allocate your time properly: each paper has six questions worth ten marks each (60 marks per paper), so spend about 10 minutes on each question.

When you are testing yourself on a paper, you may find it most effective to attempt all the questions you can before turning to Section 2 for help on those questions with which you are having difficulty. If you need more help or explanation than you find in Section 2, look up the topic in your text book or ask your teacher.

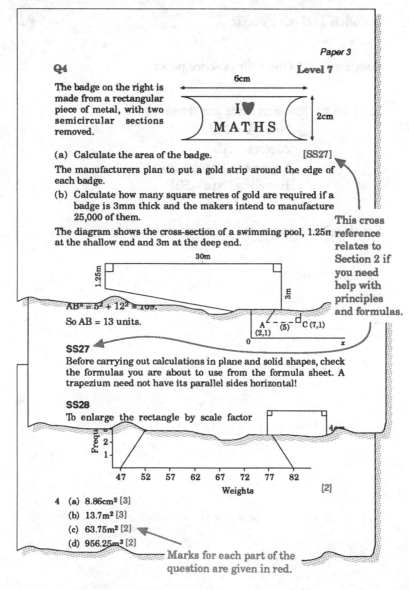

Paper 3

Q4   **Level 7**

The badge on the right is made from a rectangular piece of metal, with two semicircular sections removed.

6cm

I ♥ MATHS

2cm

(a) Calculate the area of the badge.   [SS27]

The manufacturers plan to put a gold strip around the edge of each badge.

(b) Calculate how many square metres of gold are required if a badge is 3mm thick and the makers intend to manufacture 25,000 of them.

The diagram shows the cross-section of a swimming pool, 1.25m at the shallow end and 3m at the deep end.

This cross reference relates to Section 2 if you need help with principles and formulas.

30m

1.25m

3m

$AB^2 = 5^2 + 12^2 = 169.$

So AB = 13 units.

A (2,1) — (5) — C (7,1)

0   *x*

SS27

Before carrying out calculations in plane and solid shapes, check the formulas you are about to use from the formula sheet. A trapezium need not have its parallel sides horizontal!

SS28

To enlarge the rectangle by scale factor

4cm

Frequ

2

1

47   52   57   62   67   72   77   82

Weights

[2]

4 (a) 8.86cm² [3]

  (b) 13.7m² [3]

  (c) 63.75m² [2]

  (d) 956.25m³ [2]

Marks for each part of the question are given in red.

Contents

Question analysis by topic

In each paper, Question 1 is Level 7; Question 2 is Level 8; Question 3 is Level 8; Question 4 is Level 9; Question 5 is Level 9; Question 6 is Level 10.

	Number	Algebra	Shape & Space	Handling Data
Paper 1	Q1, Q3	Q5	Q2, Q6	Q4
Paper 2	Q5	Q2, Q3	Q1, Q4	Q6
Paper 3	Q4	Q3, Q6	Q1, Q2	Q5
Paper 4	Q1	Q5, Q6	Q2	Q3, Q4
Paper 5	Q4	Q1, Q5	Q3	Q2, Q6
Paper 6	Q2, Q5	Q4, Q6	Q3	Q1
Paper 7	Q1	Q5	Q2, Q4	Q3, Q6
Paper 8	Q3	Q6	Q1, Q4	Q2, Q5
Paper 9		Q1, Q3, Q4	Q5, Q6	Q2
Paper 10	Q2	Q1, Q3	Q4, Q5	Q6
Paper 11	Q2, Q6	Q1, Q3	Q5	Q4
Paper 12		Q2, Q6	Q3, Q4, Q5	Q1
Paper 13		Q5	Q2, Q3, Q6	Q1, Q4
Paper 14	Q2	Q3, Q4	Q5, Q6	Q1
Paper 15	Q3	Q2	Q1, Q5, Q6	Q4

Section 1 – One-hour practice papers

This section consists of 15 one-hour cross-topic practice papers that together will cover the whole of the GCSE syllabus and test the Attainment Targets 2 to 5. These require written answers. The level of each question (ie Level 7, 8, 9 or 10) is indicated, and most of the questions have a 'helpline' reference to Section 2 where notes are available to assist you, eg AL7 is directing you to point 7 of the Algebra notes. Each question is worth ten marks, making each paper worth a total of 60 marks.

Paper One

Q1   Level 7

Some pupils were asked to measure the distance between 2 trees in a local park.

(a) Sam and Jill found it to be "180m to the nearest m". Copy and complete the statement: ...≤ distance < ... [NU5]

(b) Amire and Paula found it to be "179.5m to the nearest half-metre". Write a similar answer for this.

US	$4.95
CAN	$5.95
UK	£3.50

The price of a novel in three different countries is shown on the left.

Using these prices as a guide convert:

(c) US $ 1000 to sterling. [NU2]

(d) 80p in sterling into Canadian money. [NU2]

Q2   Level 8

If $\mathbf{a} = \begin{pmatrix} 2 \\ -7 \end{pmatrix}$ and $\mathbf{b} = \begin{pmatrix} 4 \\ 3 \end{pmatrix}$ find:

(a) $3\mathbf{a} + 2\mathbf{b}$ (b) k if $2\mathbf{a} + k\mathbf{b} = \begin{pmatrix} 20 \\ -2 \end{pmatrix}$

(c) m if $m\mathbf{a} + m\mathbf{b} = \begin{pmatrix} 18 \\ -12 \end{pmatrix}$

(d) the co-ordinates of the point P (1,5) after a translation 3$\mathbf{a}$.

[SS16]

1

Q3   Level 8

The table shows the masses in grammes of three entities in Litchland.

glitch	blitch	mlitch
2×10^{-4}g	5×10^{-5}g	7×10^{-9}g

(a) How many blitches are needed to weigh as much as 1 glitch? [NU4]

(b) There are 3 million mlitches; state their weight in kg. Give your answer in standard form. [NU7]

(c) How many blitches are needed to weigh a kg? Give your answer in standard form. [NU7]

(d) During an evolutionary phase the weight of the glitch became 2×10^{-3}; describe mathematically what happened to it.

Q4   Level 9

(a) What is random sampling? [HD16]

(b) In stratified sampling subgroups (subpopulations or strata) are taken into consideration. What difficulties are associated with this type of sampling?

The table below shows the number of pupils in different forms in a secondary school. You have been asked by the Head to do a sample of pupils' reading habits.

Assuming your sample to be about 70 pupils explain how you would structure it if the school is

(c) single sex;

(d) mixed.

Year	Y7	Y8	Y9	Y10	Y11	L6	U6
Number of pupils	120	120	119	120	118	60	63

Q5   Level 9

(a) Match each item from list 1 with one from list 2: [AL19]

     List 1   (i) 2^{-3} (ii) $2^3 + 2^4$ (iii) $-(64)^{1/2}$

     List 2   (i)   -8   (ii)   0.125   (iii) 3×2^3

(b) Plot the co-ordinates (x,y) from the table below and join them with a smooth curve:

x	1	1.2	1.4	1.6	1.8	2
y	0.17	0.29	0.46	0.68	0.97	1.33

(c) Draw a tangent to the graph at $x = 1.7$ and calculate its gradient.   [AL21]

(d) Given that $\dfrac{x^3}{y}$ is constant,

write down a formula connecting x and y in the form $y = \dfrac{x^3}{k}$, where k is given to 1 significant figure.   [AL18]

Q6   **Level 10**

ABCD is a cyclic quadrilateral with AD and BC produced meeting at E.

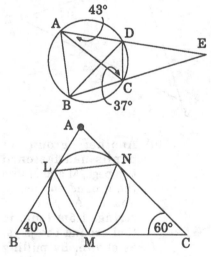

(a) Calculate the size of angle ABC   [SS24]

(b) If also EC = ED, calculate the size of angle E.   [SS24]

In the diagram the circle touches the 3 sides of ΔABC at L, M and N.

(c) Calculate the size of each angle in triangle LMN.   [SS24]

"You cannot have a cyclic parallelogram."

(d) Do you agree? [SS24]

Paper Two

Q1   **Level 7**

A school playground is paved with slabs, each a metre square and it is used to teach some mathematical topics.

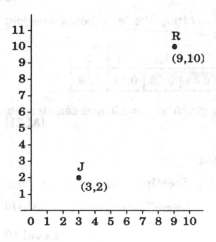

For a lesson in Geometry, Jane stands at (3,2) and Rheena stands at (9,10)

(a) **Prove that they are 10m apart.**
[SS8]

(b) Simon is told to walk in a line such that he is always equidistant from the two girls. Describe the locus of his route. [SS3]

(c) Peter is standing on a spot where he is equidistant from each girl; the angle JPR is a right angle. Calculate to the nearest metre how far he is from each girl. [SS7]

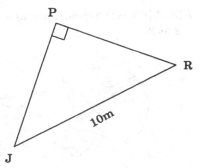

(d) Another group of pupils had fastened two pegs, M and N into the ground one metre apart. A piece of string, 1.5m long, is tied around the pegs, as shown. By pulling the string taut with a piece of chalk, and keeping it taut, they move the chalk around to draw a curve. Make a sketch of their curve. [SS5]

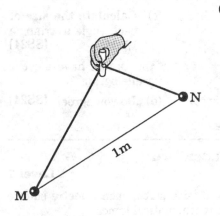

Q2 Level 8

(a) Factorise $5x^3 - 15xy$. [AL12]

A drain-cleaning company uses the formula $C = 30 + 15n$ to calculate the cost in £ for n hours work. The graph shows the relationship.

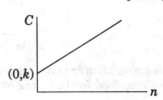

(b) Write down the value of k. [AL13]

(c) What is the gradient of the line? [AL13]

(d) Rearrange the formula to make n the subject. [AL14]

Q3 Level 8

Solve the inequalities

(a) $7n - 3 \geq 25$ [AL16]

(b) $2n^2 \leq 50$ [AL16]

(c) Draw on a pair of co-ordinates axes the graphs of $y = 2x + 3$ and $x + y = 7$. [AL8]

Shade the region satisfied by $y > 0$, $x > 0$, $y > 2x + 3$ and $x + y < 7$.

(d) Use 4 inequalities to denote the area inside the quadrilateral formed by the two axes and the two lines.

Q4 Level 9

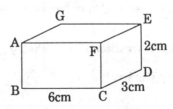

(a) In the cuboid shown calculate the size of the angle between the longest diagonal (BE) and the base. [SS17]

(b) The cuboid is placed in a cylindrical tube of the same length which just touches the edges. Calculate the length of the arc of which FE is a chord. [SS20]

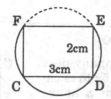

A manufacturer produces plastic covers of the type seen in cafes to keep food fresh; all the covers are similar in shape.

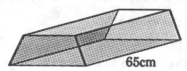

The cover above is 65cm long. The owner orders a new one to hold twice as much food.

(c) Calculate the length of the new cover. [SS19]

(d) Show that the surface area of the old cover is about 63% of the area of the new one. [SS19]

Q5 **Level 9**

(a) Choose two irrational numbers from this list

(i) Sin 30° (ii) $\sqrt{10}$ (iii) π^2 (iv) $\sqrt{6\frac{1}{4}}$ [NU11]

(b) "If you multiply two irrational numbers, the result is irrational." This statement is not always true; give a counter example.

If you multiply an irrational number by a positive integer the result is irrational.

(c) Given that $\sqrt{5}$ is irrational, show that $\sqrt{180}$ is irrational.

(d) Show that $\sqrt{162}$ is irrational.

Q6 **Level 10**

Jay keeps a record of her homework marks for English and Maths over a 10 week period (A to J)

Week	A	B	C	D	E	F	G	H	I	J
English	7	8	6	5	10	0	9	9	5	6
Maths	7	2	3	10	0	10	9	9	9	6

(a) The mean of her English marks is 6.5; calculate the standard deviation.   [HD19]

(b) The mean of her Maths marks is the same as for English, and the standard deviation is 3.44; compare her performance in the two subjects.

(c) A box contains 7 red, 9 green and 10 purple floppy disks; if 2 disks are picked at random (without replacement), what are the chances that they are the same colour?   [HD26]

(d) If a 12-sided die numbered from 1 to 12 is thrown twice, what are the chances of throwing at least one seven?
                                                                    [HD27]

Paper 3

Q1   Level 7

The badge below is made from a rectangular piece of metal, with two semicircular sections removed.

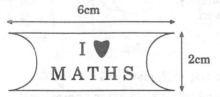

6cm

I ♥ MATHS

2cm

(a) Calculate the area of the badge.

The manufacturers plan to put a gold strip around the edge of each badge.

(b) Calculate how many square metres of gold are required if a badge is 3mm thick and the makers intend to manufacture 25,000 of them.

The diagram shows the cross-section of a swimming pool, 1.25m at the shallow end and 3m at the deep end.

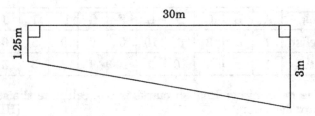

Calculate:

(c) the area of this cross-section.   [FORMULA SHEET]

(d) the volume of the pool if it is 15m long.   [SS9]

Q2   **Level 8**

A photograph of size 6cm × 10cm is to be enlarged so that the longer side is 23cm.

(a) Calculate to the nearest cm the length of the other side.   [SS10]

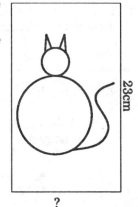

(b) Another photo has dimensions 4.5 × 7.5. Is this similar to the original? Justify your answer.

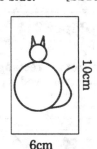

6cm   ?

The scale on a map of England is 1: 2000 000

(c) From Bristol to Nottingham is approximately 10cm on the map; calculate the true distance in km.   [SS12]

(d) From Middlesbrough to London is approximately 350km; calculate how far apart they are on the map.   [SS12]

Q3   **Level 8**

y varies as x^2; $y = 128$ when $x = 8$.

(a) Find y when $x = 4$.   [AL11]

(b) Sketch a graph of the relationship between x and y; assume x can take negative values.   [AL28]

The table below show corresponding values of a and b

a	4.8	2.4	1.6	1.2
b	5	10	15	20

(c) Write down a rule connecting a and b (assume it is a type of proportionality). [AL11]

(d) Sketch a graph of the relationship which could include negative values for a. [AL17]

Q4   Level 9

(a) If $a + b = 15$, and $a = 8 \pm \frac{1}{2}$, find b.

(b) When the number of people in the crowd at a cricket match is given as 12,000 to 3 significant figures, what is the difference between the largest and smallest possible number of people in the crowd? [NU12]

(c) What fraction is equivalent to 0.1666... recurring? [NU11]

(d) Using your answer to (c) or otherwise, find the fraction equivalent to 0.666...

Q5   Level 9

The table below shows the salaries (s) of 200 workers in a large town

Salary (£'000s)	Number	Class interval (£)	Frequency density per £1000
$7 \leq s < 8$	40	1000	40
$8 \leq s < 10$	55	2000	$27\frac{1}{2}$
$10 \leq s < 15$	75	5000	?
$15 \leq s < ?$	30	?	$7\frac{1}{2}$

(a) What figure should replace the ? in the third row? [HD12]

(b) Complete the fourth row.

(c) Draw a frequency density histogram to represent the date. [HD12]

(d) What does the area of the histogram represent? [HD13]

Q6   Level 10

The diagram shows two concentric circles, of radii r and R.

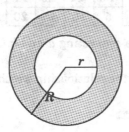

(a) Give an expression for the shaded ring in terms of r and R,
    in fully factorised form.   [AL23]

(b) If $R = 3r$, calculate the width of the ring if its area is
    $200\pi\,cm^2$.

In the given rectangle the length is 8cm more than the width.

Area = 75cm²	$x$cm

$(x+8)$cm

(c) Show that $(x + 4)^2 = 91$ [AL24]

(d) Calculate x to 2 decimal places.

Paper Four

Q1   Level 7

(a) Express 1700 as the product of prime numbers.   [NU3]

(b) Use your answer for (a) to express 8500 as the product of
    primes.   [NU3]

(c) When asked to calculate $\dfrac{1200 + 70}{5}$ an inexperienced pupil

    gave the answer 1214; set out the order in which he put the
    figures into his calculator.   [NU4]

(d) Use calculator symbols to show how $\dfrac{23 + 76 \times 48}{86 + 24}$ should be
    solved.
                                                                 [NU4]

Q2   **Level 8**

(a) Each of the expressions below describes either perimeter, area or volume. Assuming a, b, and r are linear measurements, state which is which:

    (i) $\frac{2}{3}\pi r^3$ (ii) $5\pi r^2$ (iii) $\pi(a+b)$ [SS15]

Given that $\mathbf{m} = \begin{pmatrix} 2 \\ 3 \end{pmatrix}$ and $\mathbf{n} = \begin{pmatrix} -4 \\ 4 \end{pmatrix}$

(b) write down an expression for $3\mathbf{m} - 2\mathbf{n}$

(c) under a translation the co-ordinate (1,3) moves to (7,12); describe the translation in terms of $\mathbf{m}$ and/or $\mathbf{n}$.   [SS16]

(d) What angle does the vector m make with the horizontal?
                                        [SS14]

Q3   **Level 8**

Rapid-Post promises to deliver 85% of their parcels on the day of collection.

(a) Copy and complete the tree diagram for the delivery of two parcels on the same day to different destinations.   [HD11]

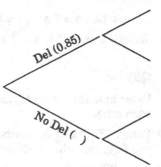

What is the probability that

(b) both parcels will be delivered?

(c) neither will be delivered?

(d) only one parcel will be delivered?

Q4   **Level 9**

In a school 60% of the boys and 80% of the girls favour having prefects. Assuming that these figures resulted from a properly conducted sample, what percentage of the children favour a prefect system if

(a) boys and girls are in equal numbers?

(b) the ratio of girls to boys is 4:1?   [HD17]

State

(c) some of the disadvantages of stratified sampling.

(d) some difficulties associated with random sampling.

Q5   Level 9

The table of results shown comes from an experiment with two variables p and q.

p	0	1	2	3	4	5
q	0	$\frac{1}{2}$	2	$4\frac{1}{2}$	8	$12\frac{1}{2}$

(a) Explain why q is not directly proportional to p.   [AL11]

(b) The experimenters think the relationship is of the form:

$$q = ap^n$$

By making appropriate substitutions calculate a and n.   [AL18]

In another experiment variable r and s were found to be connected by the rule

$$s = \frac{a}{r^n} \qquad (r \neq 0)$$

Calculate

(c) s when $a = 7$ and $n = 0$

(d) s when $r = 64$, $n = \frac{2}{3}$ and $a = 7$ [AL10]

Q6   Level 10

Peter and Jane are playing 'think of a number' type games with each other:

Peter: "Think of a number and square it; add on the number you first thought of. Result?"

Jane: "Thirty."

(a) Let n be Jane's number. Form an equation in n and make it equal to zero.

(b) Solve your equation to find 2 possible numbers Jane could have thought of.   [AL24]

It is now Jane's turn:

Jane: "Think of a number; add three to it and find the reciprocal of your answer; go back to your original number and add four to it; take the reciprocal of this and add your two answers together. Result?"

Peter: "Nine-twentieths".

(c) Let n be Peter's number. Form an equation to express his result and combine your 2 algebraic fractions into a single fraction. [AL25]

(d) Your equation reduces to $9n^2 - 23n - 32 = 0$; solve this equation to find the whole number Peter thought of.
[AL24]

Paper Five

Q1 Level 7

Paula leaves home to visit a friend in Xtown; she travels at 30mph for one hour, stops for a half-hour break, then travels the last 45 miles at the same speed as she did the first part of her journey.

(a) Assuming she left at 9a.m., draw a travel graph to describe Paula's journey.

(b) When would a cyclist, who left Xtown at 9.30a.m. and travelled at 15mph meet Paula?

In the inequalities below, list the values of n.

(c) $-4 \leq n < 3$, n is an integer. [AL5]

(d) $-4 \leq n < 3$ and $-10 \leq n < -1$, n is an integer.

Q2 Level 8

The graph below shows the cumulative frequency of the salaries for 30 employees in a small factory. Using the graph, calculate

(a) the lower quartile

(b) the upper quartile

(c) the median and

(d) the interquartile range. [HD10]

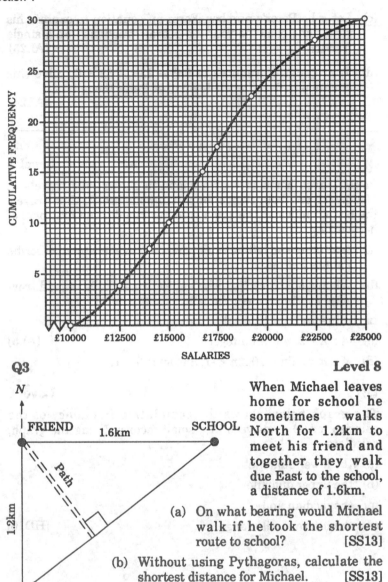

Q3   **Level 8**

When Michael leaves home for school he sometimes walks North for 1.2km to meet his friend and together they walk due East to the school, a distance of 1.6km.

(a) On what bearing would Michael walk if he took the shortest route to school?   [SS13]

(b) Without using Pythagoras, calculate the shortest distance for Michael.   [SS13]

Sometimes his friend walks along the dotted path to meet Michael on the direct route:

(c) Calculate the length of the path.

(d) Calculate the bearing on which the friend walks.

14

Q4 **Level 9**

(a) Which of the numbers in this set are irrational? [NU11]
$$3.14, \pi, 0.\dot{8}, \sqrt{2}+1+1, \sqrt{289}$$

(b) Multiply out the following, and simplify your answer
$$(\sqrt{2}+1)(\sqrt{2}-1)$$

(c) Using your answer to (b) simplify $(\sqrt{2}+1)^8(\sqrt{2}-1)^8$

(d) Without using a calculator simplify the expression
$$\frac{\sqrt{75}+\sqrt{27}}{\sqrt{12}}$$
(make your method clear)

Q5 **Level 9**

Given that $y = 2^x$,

(a) complete the table of values on the right.

x	0	0.5	1	1.5	2	2.5	3
y	1	1.4					

(b) choose suitable axes and draw the graph of the relationship between x and y; draw a tangent at the point where $x = 1.8$, and calculate its gradient. [AL21]

By drawing appropriate graphs on the same axes solve as accurately as your graphs allow, the equations:

(c) $2^x - 3.4 = 0$ [AL20]

(d) $y = \dfrac{1}{x}$

Q6 **Level 10**

(a) In the diagram below, the jobs in an operation are circled, and the time in minutes for each is written on the arrows. Calculate the completion time of the operation. [HD22]

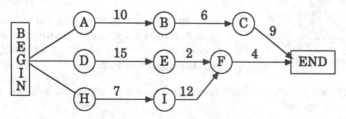

15

(b) Write a short sentence to describe the clusters of arrows in this part of a network relating to tasks *a,b...f*.

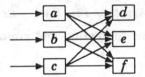

Criticise the diagrams below – times are not given and are not necessary.

(c)

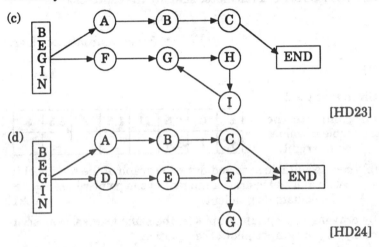

[HD23]

(d)

[HD24]

Paper Six

Q1   Level 7

In an experiment on probability a class used the spinner shown below

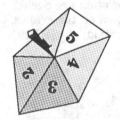

(a) How many times would you expect it to land on 2, if it were spun 130 times?
[HD8]

(b) Lucy and Paul informed the class that it came down on 'even numbers 96 times'; how many times are they likely to have spun their spinner? [HD9]

Another group of children recorded their results in a table as shown below:

Result	1	2	3	4	5
Times	20	30	20	29	21

(c) What appears to be the probability of getting an even number with their spinner? [HD8]

(d) Comment on your answer.

Q2   Level 8

In 1978 the population of Rwanda was 4,198,000.

(a) Express this figure in standard index form to two significant figures. [NU7]

(b) The density of population per sq/km was 159. Calculate the area of the country in sq/kms giving your answer in standard index form. [NU7]

Express the answers which result from the calculations below in standard index form:

(c) $\dfrac{1}{1,000} + \dfrac{1}{5,000}$ [NU7]

(d) $(0.00000005)^2$ [NU7]

Q3   Level 8

The diagram shows the route of a boat which leaves a port (P) and sails 25km on a bearing 070°; it then sails due South for 5 km to the cove (C).

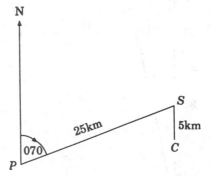

Calculate

(a) how far S is north of P. [SS13]

(b) how far S is east of P. [SS13]

(c) the bearing of C from P. [SS14]

(d) using your answer to (c) calculate the distance PC. You must use trigonometry. [SS13]

Q4   **Level 9**

The graph shows the height of a stone thrown upwards over a 10 second interval;

(a) What is the velocity of the stone at $t = 3$ sec?   [AL21]

(b) What is the velocity of the stone at $t = 7$ sec?

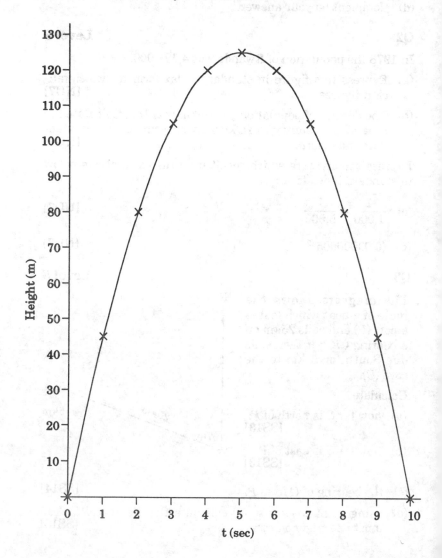

The diagram shows part of a cyclist's journey;

(c) Calculate her acceleration over the first five seconds.

[AL21]

(d) From the 20th second she decelerates uniformly at the rate of $2\frac{1}{2}$ m/s^{-2} until she comes to a halt. For how long was she in motion altogether?

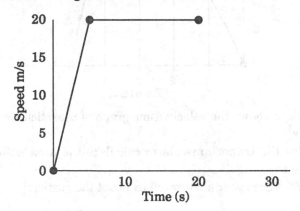

Q5   **Level 9**

$\dfrac{1}{a}$ is a fraction with $1 < a < 10$

(a) Write down the values of a which give recurring decimals.

[NU11]

(b) If $10 < b < 20$,

which fraction of the form $\dfrac{1}{b}$ has a finite decimal?

(c) A pupil has correctly given an answer as 5.30, where 5.3 would have been wrong; write down a possible answer she had before rounding and the degree of accuracy required.

(d) A piece of piping measures 20m ± 5cm; if 17 pieces are laid in a straight line, what is the difference in length between the longest and shortest possible line of pipes?   [NU14]

Q6   **Level 10**

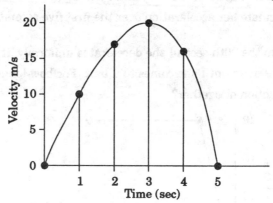

The graph shows the velocity/time graph of a particle over a 5s interval.

(a) Use the trapezium rule to calculate the area under the curve.   [AL27]

(b) What does your answer tell us about the particle?

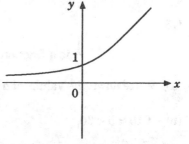

The graph of a function is shown on the left; make two neat sketches to show

(c) $y = f(x) - 1$ [AL28]

(d) $y = \dfrac{1}{f(x)}$ [AL28]

Paper Seven

Q1   **Level 7**

There are 28.4g in an ounce and 16 ounces in a pound.

Using these facts change

(a) 9.94kg to pounds.

(b) 71 stones to kilograms, given additionally that there are 14 pounds in a stone.   [NU2]

Given that 1 inch = 2.54cm and 12 inches = 1 foot, convert

(c) 2 feet 3 inches to cm.

(d) 50.8m to feet (giving your answer to the nearest foot)

[NU2]

Q2   Level 8

(a) Which of the following statements are true?

   (i) all circles are similar to each other

   (ii) all rectangles are similar to each other

   (iii) all squares are similar to each other.

(b) The Choco label measures 6cm × 4cm; for a public advertisement the makers uses an enlarged version 1.5m long. Calculate the width of the new poster. [SS11]

The diagrams below refer to the same box; diagram (i) is a plan showing two equal non-overlapping flaps, with diagram (ii) showing the box from the side with the flaps opened out.

(i)

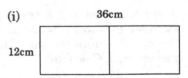

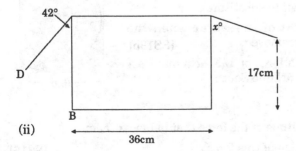

(ii)

21

Given that the box is 30cm deep calculate

(c)   the angle marked 'x'   [SS14]

(d)   the length of the line DB.

(Hint: make DB the hypotenuse of a right angled triangle.)

[SS14]

Q3   Level 8

Class Y9 is asked to investigate the possible outcomes when 3 coins are tossed; Joel's group lists all the outcomes starting with H, H, H.

(a)   List all the possible outcomes.

(b)   Use your table to state the probability of getting at least two heads when three coins are tossed.

Paul's group decides to draw a tree diagram to illustrate the possible outcomes:

(c)   Copy and complete their tree diagram.   [HD11]

(d)   Use the tree diagram to calculate the probability of getting at least two heads.

1st TOSS

H   ($\frac{1}{2}$)

T   ($\frac{1}{2}$)

Q4   Level 9

A sphere of radius 3 cm is placed in a cylinder as shown; water is poured into the cylinder until the top of the sphere is just covered. Calculate

(a)   the volume of the sphere. (You are advised not to substitute for π)

(b)   the height of the water when the sphere is removed.   [SS19b]

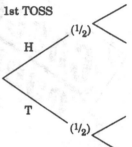

— 6cm —

On an object a force of 12N acts due East and a force of 5N due South.

Calculate:

(c)   the magnitude of the force that balances them

(d)   the direction of this force.   [SS16]

Q5   **Level 9**

W_0	W_1	W_2
5×10^6	1.5×10^7	4.5×10^7

The table shows the number of microbes in a jar over a 3 week observation period; it is known that the colony has increased and will continue to increase at the same rate.

(a) If $W_n = 3^4 \times 5 \times 10^6$, state the value of n.

(b) Write down an expression for the number of microbes during W_x.

(c) Write down an expression, similar to the one in (a), for the number of microbes two weeks prior to the start of the observation.   [AL19]

(d) Use your calculator to estimate the age of the colony.

Q6   **Level 10**

(a) The graphs show the performances of teams Y7 and Y8 in the 'long-kick' competition. Comment on the graphs.   [HD20]

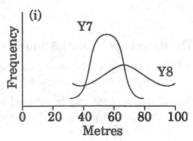

In diagrams (ii) and (iii) the mean is 20.

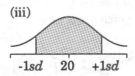

(b) If the distribution in diagram (ii) is normal, give the standard deviation.   [HD21]

(c) Approximately what percentage of the area under the curve in diagram (iii) is shaded if it is part of a normal distribution curve?   [HD21]

(d) The standard deviation of d_1, d_2, d_3, d_4...d_n is 12; state the standard deviation of

(i) $4d_1$, $4d_2$,...$4d_n$

(ii) $5d_1 + 1$, $5d_2 + 1$,...$5d_n + 1$

Paper Eight

Q1   **Level 7**

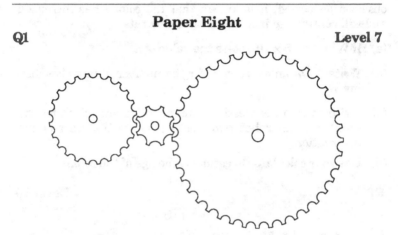

The three cogs have 24,8 and 40 teeth respectively.

(a) how many turns must each cog make before they are lined up again as they started?   [SS6]

(b) If the largest cog is rotated anti-clockwise at the rate of 90 revolutions per minute, describe what happens to the cog on the left.   [SS6]

The diagrams in (c) and (d) show wheels connected by belts, some of which are crossed.

(c)   (d)

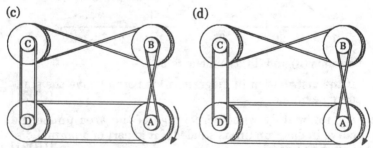

Describe what happens to wheels B, C and D if wheel A is turned clockwise.

Q2   **Level 8**

Class Y7 is asked by their teacher to design a questionnaire to test the hypothesis that 'religious people have larger families'.

Joseph's group include the question 'do you have children?'

(a) Criticise this question and suggest a better method of expressing it.

(b) Criticise the wording of the original hypothesis.   [HD1]

The children in the class volunteer to distribute the questionnaire to all the houses in their areas.

(c) State why this has an advantage over face-to-face interviews.

(d) State a disadvantage of conducting the survey in this way.

Q3   **Level 8**

(a) Express 128 as a power of 2.   [NU3]

(b) Simplify $125^{1/3}$.   [NU6]

(c) Use the formula $A = P + \dfrac{PRT}{100}$ to evaluate A when

    $P = £5,000, R = 7\frac{3}{8}\%, T = 4$ years.   [NU9]

(d) In the formula $K = m^2 - n^2$, find K when $m = -7$ and $n = -6\frac{3}{4}$.   [NU8]

Q4   **Level 9**

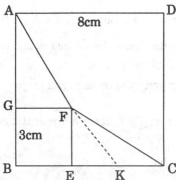

The diagram shows two squares of sides 8cm and 3cm, having a common vertex B.

(a) Prove that triangles AGF and CEF are congruent.   [SS18]

AF extended meets BC at K. Write down the value of

(b) Sin G$\hat{\text{F}}$K

(c) Cos G$\hat{\text{F}}$K

(d) Tan G$\hat{\text{F}}$K   [SS21]

Q5   **Level 9**

A pupil shuffles a pack of ordinary playing cards.

(a) What are the chances she will draw a red card followed by a red card, assuming she does not replace the first one?
                                           [HD18]

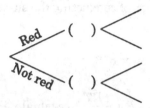

(b) Copy and complete the tree diagram above to illustrate how she could select the two cards.

(c) What are the chances her second card is a red card?

(d) What are the chances both her selections are the same colour?   [HD26]

Q6   **Level 10**

Consider the iterative equation $x_{n+1} = \sqrt{6x_n + 7}$

(a) Let $x_1 = 6$; write down the values of x_2, x_3, x_4, giving your answers to 2 decimal places.   [AL22]

(b) State whether your sequence is converging or diverging.
                                           [AL22]

(c) By letting $x_n = x_{n+1} = r$, form a quadratic equation in r and solve it.   [AL22]

(d) Show clearly that

$$x_{n+1} = \frac{7}{x_n - 6}$$

is another iterative formula for your equation in (c). [AL22]

Paper Nine

Q1   **Level 7**

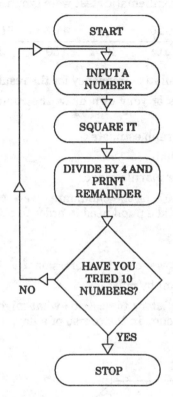

(a) What is printed if 10 is the input?   [AL9]

(b) If you input many different numbers, what figures will be printed?

   (You might try all the numbers from 1 to 10, for example.)
                                                              [AL9]

In Miss Hussein's cupboard there are 50 textbooks, some Inter-mediate Level, the rest Higher. The total value of the books is £290.

(c) If an Intermediate book costs £5 and a Higher one £7, form two simultaneous equations in I and H.

(d) Solve your equations to find how many Higher books she has.   [AL7]

Q2   **Level 8**

The results of a mathematics test were grouped as below:

MARKS	1-20	21-40	41-60	61-80	81-100
FREQ.	10	20	30	25	15

(a) Make a cumulative frequency for the results.

(b) Using scales of your own draw the cumulative frequency graph.

(c) From your graph estimate

    (i) the median   [HD10]

    (ii) the interquartile range.   [HD10]

(d) If the top 20% of the candidates were awarded grade A, what mark did a pupil need in order to get A?

Q3   **Level 8**

(a) Write as a power of y the expression $\sqrt[3]{y}$ [AL10]

(b) What is meant by $m^{3/2}$?   [AL10]

(c) Write a *brief* story to describe what might have happened to Peter's money in the course of a day, using the graph as a guide: [AL17]

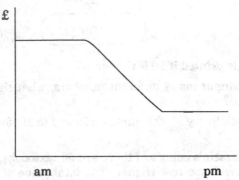

(d) Rearrange the formula $V = \frac{1}{3}\pi r^2 h$, to make h the subject.

[AL14]

Q4   **Level 9**

(a) For the relationship $y = x^3 - 7$, complete the table of values below:

x	0	1	2	2.5
y	-7			

(b) Draw a graph of the (x,y) values and use it to solve the equation

$$x^3 - 7 = x \qquad \text{[AL20]}$$

(c) Draw a tangent to the curve at the point where $x = 1$, and estimate the gradient at that point.   [AL21]

(d) Show that the equation $x^{-3}(y + 7) = 1$, is equivalent to the equation in part (a).

Q5   **Level 9**

The diagram shows a regular tetrahedron of edge 6.5cm, made from 4 pieces of plastic.

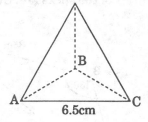

(a) Sketch one of the faces and find the length of its median.

(b) The perpendicular from the 'top' meets the base at 0; calculate the length of OX.

(c) Use trigonometry to calculate the angle between two faces.
                                                              [SS17]

(d) Another tetrahedron is made from 16 pieces of the same size as the smaller tetrahedron; write down the ratio of the volumes of the smaller to the larger tetrahedron.   [SS19]

Q6   **Level 10**

During sportsday pupils are asked to pass under two sticks, one of 2.1m and the other of 1.6m tied together as shown in the diagram.

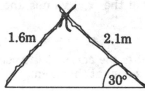

(a) Calculate the angle which the shorter stick makes with the ground.   [SS25]

(b) Use your answer to part (a) to find how far apart the ends of the sticks are. Give your answer to 1 significant figure.
[SS25]

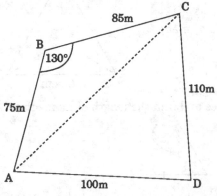

The field in which the sports take place is shown on the left.

(c) Calculate the length of the diagonal AC. [SS27]

(d) Calculate the size of angle D.   [SS26]

Paper Ten

Q1   **Level 7**

What is the *n*th term of the sequences below?

(a) 3, 7, 11, 15,...   [AL2]

(b) 0, 3, 8, 15, 24,...   [AL2]

The following sequence of numbers 0, 6, 24,... arose from a mathematical investigation.

(c) By examining the differences between the terms, as shown, write down the next two terms of the sequence:

[AL2]

(d) A teacher asked a class to find the nth term in the sequence above, advising them to express each term of the sequence as the product of consecutive numbers. Can you find the general term?

Q2   **Level 8**

The Chinook Computer's draughts programme can analyse three million moves in a minute.

Write in standard form

(a) how many moves it could analyse in an hour.   [NU7]

(b) how long, in seconds, it takes to analyse one move.   [NU7]

Simplify the following giving your answer in standard form:

(c) $\dfrac{3 \times 10^{-4} \times 4 \times 10^{7}}{6 \times 10^{-9}}$

(d) $\dfrac{3 \times 10^{-7} \div 4 \times 10^{8}}{3 \times 10^{-9} \times 8 \times 10^{-4}}$ [NU4 & NU7]

Q3   **Level 8**

(a) Find the common factors $7x^2 - 56xy$ [AL12]

(b) The volume of a cylinder is $V = \pi r^2 h$

Rearrange the formula to make r the subject.   [AL14]

(c) The volume of a sphere is $V = \frac{4}{3}\pi r^3$;

calculate r when $V = 700\text{cm}^3$.   [AL14]

(d) Multiply out the brackets and simplify your expression:

$$(9x - 15)(9x + 15)$$ [AL15]

Q4 **Level 9**

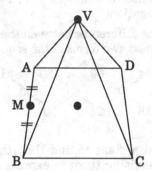

The diagram shows a square based pyramid; the apex, V, is directly above the centre of the base. AB = 13cm and VA = 20cm; M is the midpoint of AB.

(a) Calculate VM. [SS17]

(b) Calculate the size of the angle between one of the slant faces and the base. [SS17]

(c) Calculate the volume of the pyramid.

($V = \frac{1}{3} \times$ area of base $\times$ height.)

Give your answer to 1 significant figure.

(d) The pyramid is a model of a larger pyramid on a scale 1 to 40; complete this statement:

area of model : area of original = 1:_____ [SS19]

Q5 **Level 9**

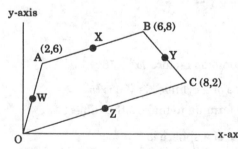

The diagram shows a quadrilateral ABCD with midpoints W, X, Y and Z.

(a) Give in the form $\begin{pmatrix} a \\ b \end{pmatrix}$ vectors for $\overrightarrow{AC}$ and $\overrightarrow{OB}$

(b) State $\overrightarrow{WX}$ in the same way.

(c) What is the relationship between WX and OB?

(d) Prove that WXYZ is a parallelogram.

Q6   **Level 10**

OFFICERENT has two types of floor space available: type A costs £10 per m^2, type B costs £15 per m^2.

If you want to hire floor space you must rent no more than 1700m^2 and pay at least £18,000 for your hired space.   [HD25]

(a) Write down an inequality in A and B to describe the floor area available.

(b) Write down and simplify an inequality to describe the cost.

(c) On a pair of co-ordinate axes draw two lines and shade suitable regions to illustrate your inequalities.

(d) Under the conditions imposed what is the largest amount of floor space you can rent for the least cost?

Paper Eleven

Q1   **Level 7**

(a) To solve the equation $y^5 = 140$, Sita used a table as the one on the right:

Try	Too big	Too small
3	✔	
2		✔

Continue Sita's table until you have found y correct to 1 decimal place.   [AL6]

(b) Simplify $\dfrac{5^4 \times 5^6}{5^8}$ giving your answer as a whole number.

[AL3]

(c) Solve the simultaneous equations: $2x - 3y = 5$ and $5x + 4y = 1$.   [AL7]

(d) Draw the graphs of the straight lines $x + y = 6$, and $y = x + 4$. Hence write down solutions to these equations.
[AL8]

Q2   Level 8

A formula for finding the area of a triangle when the three sides a, b and c are known is Area = $\sqrt{s\,(s-a)\,(s-b)\,(s-c)}$,

where $s = \dfrac{a+b+c}{2}$

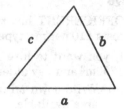

If a = 8cm, b = 15cm, c = 17cm calculate

(a) s

(b) the area of the triangle.

In the formula $P = s - \frac{1}{2}t^2$, calculate

(c) P when s = -40 and t = 3.   [NU9]

(d) P when $s = \frac{7}{8}$ and $t = \frac{3}{8}$ [NU9]

Q3   Level 8

y varies inversely as the square of x; if y = 16 when $x = \frac{1}{2}$, calculate

(a) y when $x = \frac{1}{4}$ [AL11]

(b) x when y = 0.01   [AL11]

(c) Draw and label a portion of the number line to show the inequality

$$-3 \le x < 4$$ [AL5]

(d) Write down pairs of whole numbers which satisfy all three of the statements: $y < 10$, $x > 7$ and $x + y = 12$

Q4   Level 9

The Headteacher of your school has asked you to investigate reading habits among first year pupils. There are 7 forms in the year with 30 pupils per form. You do not have enough time to question every pupil so you select one form to do your survey.

(a) Under what circumstances would your method be reasonable?

(b) Under what circumstances would your method be faulty?

The Headteacher also asks the Head Prefect to 'sound out the Sixth Form on redecorating the common room'. He will only redecorate if there is a majority in favour. The Head Prefect reports back "80% of the boys sampled and 30% of the girls are in favour, which is an average of 55%; you can therefore proceed".

(c) Under what circumstances would the Prefect's 55% be accurate?   [HD17]

(d) There are in fact 200 students in the Sixth Form; if the percentages of boys and girls in favour of change are as the Prefect suggests, calculate how many boys and how many girls are in the Sixth Form, given that only $32\frac{1}{2}$% of them want change.   [HD17]

Q5   Level 9

(a) Sin $\hat{B}$ = 0.6; give two values of $\hat{B}$ between 0° and 360°.
                                                                   [SS22]

(b) Given that 0° ≤ x ≤ 75°, draw a graph of y = 10 Tan $x°$; hence solve the equation 10 Tan $x°$ = 30° − x [SS23]

In the diagram ABCD is a square and EAB an equilateral triangle. F is the midpoint of DC.

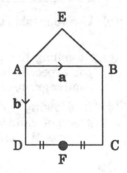

$\overrightarrow{AB}$ = **a** and $\overrightarrow{AD}$ = **b**.

Calculate vector expressions for

(c) $\overrightarrow{EF}$

(d) $\overrightarrow{DE}$ [SS16]

Q6   Level 10

If a = 3.9 and b = 4.5, with each number expressed to 2 significant figures, calculate

(a) the minimum value of $b - a$.　　　　　　　　　　[NU13]

(b) the difference between the largest and smallest values of ab.　　　　　　　　　　　　　　　　　　　　　[NU13]

(c) If $1.63 \leq x \leq 3.25$, express x in the form $c \pm d$.　[NU15]

(d) The length of a metal rod is given as 5.55m ± 5cm; what is the percentage error?　　　　　　　　　　　　[NU14]

Paper Twelve

Q1　　　　　　　　　　　　　　　　　　　　　**Level 7**

The heights of a group of children are given in cm as follows:

122, 134, 132, 154, 167, 153, 155, 126, 144, 134, 128, 153, 156, 138, 148, 163, 140, 155, 168, 148.

Sort the data into groups as follows:

Height	120–129	130–139	140–149	150–159	160–169
Frequency					

(b) Use your table to estimate the mean height of the children.　　　　　　　　　　　　　　　　　　　　　[HD2]

(c) Assuming this group is typical, how many children would you expect to have heights in the range 150cm-159cm in a similar group of 180 children?　　　　　　　　[HD8]

(d) In drawing up a questionnaire to find the heights, one group of children asked the question 'how tall are you?'. Criticise this and suggest an improvement.　　　　[HD1]

Q2　　　　　　　　　　　　　　　　　　　　　**Level 8**

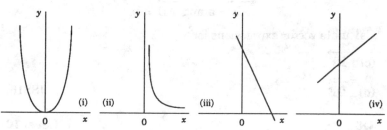

Of the 4 graphs shown which one is

(a) $y + x = 6$

(b) $y = \dfrac{3}{x}$

(c) $y = 3x^2$

(d) $y = 3x + 2$? [AL17]

Q3 **Level 8**

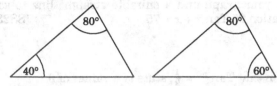

(a) Explain why the two triangles shown are similar.

(b) The two triangles shown below are similar; calculate the length of the sides marked x and y. [SS11]

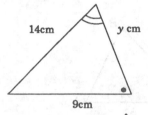 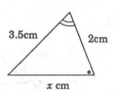

ABCD is a rectangle with $\hat{CAD} = 22.6°$; using trigonometry calculate

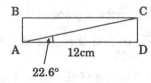

(c) the length of CD. [SS13]

(d) the length of AC. [SS13]

Q4 **Level 9**

The graph shows $y = \mathrm{Sin}\, x$ for $0 \le x \le 360$.

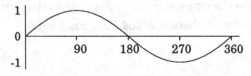

Section 1

Sketch the graph of

(a) $y = 3 \sin x$ [SS23]

(b) $y = \sin \frac{x}{2}$ [SS23]

(c) Using values of x from $0 \le x \le 75$, draw the graph of $y = \tan x$.   [SS23]

(d) Use your graph and a suitable straight line to solve the equation $25 \tan x + x = 75$.   [SS23/AL28]

Q5   **Level 9**

(a) Given that $\tan \theta° = \frac{1}{2}$, state two values of θ.   [SS22]

(b) If $\sin a° = \sin 210°$, write down a value of a where $270° < a < 360°$.   [SS22]

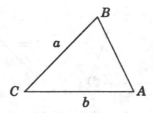

A formula for the area of a triangle is:

$$\text{Area} = \frac{1}{2} ab \sin C$$

(c) Use the formula to find the area of a triangle where $a = 3$cm, $b = 4$cm, $C = 30°$.

(d) Sketch another triangle of the same area, with the sides a and b unchanged in length.   [SS21]

Q6   **Level 10**

(a) Simplify $\dfrac{x^2 - 9}{x^2 - x - 6}$ [AL23]

(b) Rewrite the expression $4x^2 - 20x + 42$ in the form $(ax + b)^2 + c$, where a, b and c are constants.   [AL26]

The photograph in the diagram takes up 60% of the card;

(c) Make an equation in x for the area of the photograph.

(d) Solve your equation by the quadratic formula giving x to the nearest 0.01mm. [AL24]

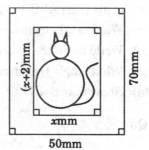

Paper Thirteen

Q1 Level 7

(a) Construct a flow diagram to calculate the mean weight of 30 people; assume the weights are being fed in one at a time. [HD6]

The table below shows the corresponding weights and heights of a group of children:

W (kg)	21	22	22	23	23	24	24	25	25	26
H (cm)	120	124	126	130	138	137	130	134	138	135

(b) Draw a scatter graph for the table.

(c) Draw the line of best fit. [HD7]

(d) The range of the weights of another group of children is the same as for the group above. Can we say anything about this second group's heights? [HD4]

Q2 Level 8

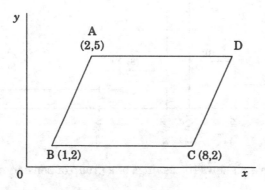

In the diagram ABCD is a parallelogram.

(a) What single transformation maps AB → DC?

(b) Write down the co-ordinates of D.

(c) What single transformation maps AD → BC?

(d) Show that $\hat{B}$ = 71.6°   [SS14]

Q3   **Level 8**

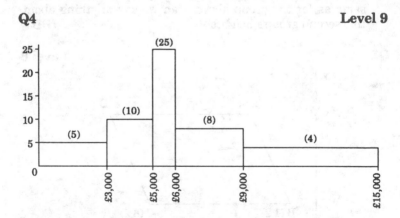

The diagram shows a cuboid of dimensions a, b, c. State which aspects of the box the expressions below describe:

(a) abc

(b) $2(ab + ac + bc)$

(c) $4(a + b + c)$

(d) $\sqrt{a^2 + b^2}$ [SS15]

Q4   **Level 9**

The histogram shows the savings of a group of pensioners.

(a) Complete the frequency table. [HD12]

Savings (£)	0-2999	3000-4999	5000-5999	6000-8999	9000-14999
Frequency	15				

(b) What does the area of the histogram represent? [HD13]

(c) Explain how the median can be estimated from the *histogram*. [HD15]

(d) Calculate the median, commenting on its accuracy. [HD15]

Q5 **Level 9**

(a) Solve the equation: $3^k \times 3^{3/4} = 9^{1/2}$.

(b) By writing each part of the following equation as a power of 2, find y:

$$\tfrac{1}{64} \times 16^y = 8. \qquad \text{[AL19]}$$

An investment with Goodhouse Building Society grows at the rate of 7% p.a.

(c) Write down the *rate* at which the investment is growing.

(d) If the initial investment was £P, write down an expression for its value after n years.

Q6 **Level 10**

(a) What single transformation is equivalent to a reflection in the x-axis followed by a reflection in the line $y = x$? [SS28]

(b) What single transformation is equivalent to a rotation of 90° anticlockwise, followed by a reflection in the y-axis? [SS28]

(c) Define the transformation which the matrix $\begin{pmatrix} 2 & 0 \\ 0 & 2 \end{pmatrix}$ represents? [SS30]

(d) What combination of transformations does the matrix $\begin{pmatrix} 0 & -2 \\ -2 & 0 \end{pmatrix}$ represent? [SS30]

Paper Fourteen

Q1 **Level 7**

The marks in a test were recorded as follows:

MARKS	MIDPOINT	FREQUENCY
0-9		1
10-19		5
20-29		12
30-39		5
40-49		7

(a) Complete the midpoint column.

(b) Calculate the mean mark. [HD2]

(c) Draw a frequency polygon to illustrate the results. [HD5]

(d) The class did better in a later test; draw a second polygon on the same axes to suggest an improvement.

Q2 **Level 8**

(a) Express 729 as a power of 3. [NU3]

(b) When a ball is dropped from a height of 1m it bounces up to $\frac{3}{4}$ of the height from which it came.

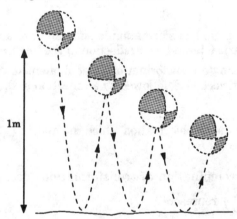

1m

Calculate how far it will have travelled when it touches the ground for the third time.

A pupil has written down $27 \times (0.8)^3 \approx 52.7$

(c) Explain why this could not be right. Do not use a calculator. [NU1]

(d) Suggest what the pupil did, if in fact 52.7 is a rounded off answer from her calculator. [NU1]

Q3 **Level 8**

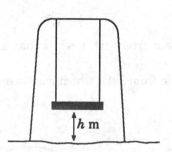

(a) Sketch a graph which describes the movements of a child's swing; put time on the horizontal axis.

Given the inequalities $3x + 3 \geq 37 > 2x + 4$

(b) what is the smallest integer value of x? [AL16]

(c) what is the largest integer value of x? [AL16]

(d) Given that $y^2 \leq 36$, state the integer values of y which satisfy this inequality. [AL16]

Q4 **Level 9**

In a scientific experiment involving two variables a and b, the following results were noticed:

b	0	1	1.1	1.2	1.5	2
a	0	3	4.0	5.2	10.0	24

From past experiences the experimenters suspect the variables are connected by the formula $a = kb^n$, where k and n are integer constants.

(a) Calculate k, by making suitable substitutions for a and b. [AL18]

(b) Use result from (a) to calculate n.

Given below are two lists of expressions:

List 1	List 2
(i) $x^{-1/2}$	(a) $b^{-1}x^4$
(ii) $\dfrac{b}{x^4}$	(b) $\dfrac{1}{\sqrt{x}}$
(iii) $\sqrt[3]{x^2}$	(c) $x^{3/2}$

(c) Choose an item from list 1 which has an equivalent in list 2.   [AL19]

(d) Choose an item from list 1 which has its reciprocal in list 2.   [AL4]

Q5   **Level 9**

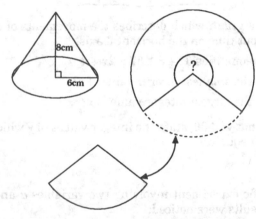

The diagram shows a small conical hat a child had made for a doll. The net is shown next to it.

(a) Calculate the perimeter of the net, giving your answer to 1 decimal place.

(b) Calculate the angle of the sector.   [SS20]

A second had was made with the remaining sector. Express in simplest terms

(c) the ratio of the surface area of the larger hat to that of the smaller one: [SS20]

(d) the ratio of the volume of the larger hat to that of the smaller one.

Q6   **Level 10**

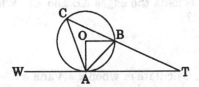

In the diagram TA is a tangent to the circle, O is the centre and OAB is an equilateral triangle.

(a) Write down the size of angle C.   [SS24]

(b) If angle CÂW = 75°, calculate the size of angle CB̂O.
                                                       [SS24]

(c) If TW = TC, calculate the size of angle TŴC.

(d) If TA = 12cm, TB = 9cm, calculate CB.   [SS24]

Paper Fifteen

Q1   **Level 7**

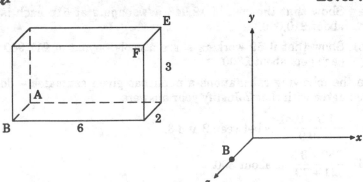

The cuboid (shown above left) has dimensions 6 by 2 by 3 units. It is placed on the axes (above right) such that the corner marked A is on the origin and the edges just touch the axes.

(a) What are the co-ordinates of the vertex marked F?   [SS1]

(b) What is the length of the diagonal of the base of the cuboid? Give your answer to the nearest 0.1.   [SS7]

(c) Describe the locus of points which are equidistant from F and E.   [SS4]

(d) A flat sheet of metal is used to divide the box into two compartments; it joins the edges AB and EF. What is the area of this sheet? [SS7]

Q2 Level 8

(a) $x = m^2 - n^2$. Calculate m when $x = 4$ and $n = -1\frac{1}{2}$. [AL14]

(b) Factorise the expression $4x^2 + 8xy$. [AL12]

(c) Rearrange the formula $n = v - mx^2$, to make x the subject. [AL14]

(d) In the formula $k^2 = 100 - m^2$, what are the largest and smallest numerical values m can have if k is a real number?

Q3 Level 8

In this question you are asked to estimate; do not use a calculator. [NU1 & NU10]

(a) Show that the cost of 19,946 newspapers at 51p each is about £10,000.

(b) Show that if 59 workers share a pools payout of £17,900, each gets about £300.

In the following calculations a pupil has given estimates – do you agree with them? Justify your answers.

(c) $\dfrac{71.9 \times 0.81}{19.9}$ is between 2 and 3.

(d) $\dfrac{760 \times 3.9}{21 + 79}$ is about 300.

(No credit will be given for calculator methods.)

Q4 Level 9

The frequency table show the distribution of marks in a test

Marks	16-19	20-23	24-31	32-43
Frequency	5	4	12	9

(a) Using a standard width of 4 draw a histogram to show the distribution. [HD12]

(b) How many pupils scored below 27? [HD15]

(c) What was the modal group of marks? [HD3]

(d) If the third and fourth groups of marks were combined into one, what would be the height of the column representing it?

Q5 **Level 9**

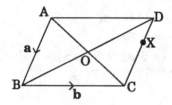

ABCD is a parallelogram with $\overrightarrow{AB}$ = **a** and $\overrightarrow{BC}$ = **b**

Write down in terms of a and b

(a) $\overrightarrow{AC}$

(b) $\overrightarrow{OX}$, where X is a point such that $\overrightarrow{DX} = \tfrac{1}{2}\overrightarrow{XC}$ [SS16]

An air pilot wishes to fly due North but there is a wind of 50mph blowing from the West. If the plane can fly at 300mph,

(c) sketch a vector diagram and use it to find the bearing on which the pilot should fly;

(d) the true speed of the aircraft relative to the ground. [SS16]

Q6 **Level 10**

Write down a matrix equivalent to: [SS30]

(a) reflection in the x-axis.

(b) an enlargement scale factor $\tfrac{1}{2}$, centre (0,0]

(c) Rotation 90° clockwise about the origin.

(d) The inverse of a reflection in the line $y = x$. [SS29]

Section 2 – Revision notes and formulas

> This section contains a brief summary of the essential mathematical principles and formulas of the GCSE syllabus, with examples where necessary, organised by topic:
>
> ❑ NU = Number,
>
> ❑ AL = Algebra,
>
> ❑ SS = Shape and Space,
>
> ❑ HD = Handling Data.
>
> These notes can be used to help with specific questions, or independently as revision notes.

Number

NU1

$7600 \times 0.8 < 7600$ while $7600 \div 0.8 > 7600$; when you multiply a quantity by a number less than 1, it decreases. The reverse is true for division.

NU2

When a question has more than one part, you are often asked to write down a part-answer to a given degree of accuracy. In subsequent parts of the question where the part-answer is used, it is more accurate to work with the unrounded value, so *do not clear your calculator display until you are sure you no longer require it.*

Example: 598 books cost £4760. Calculate the cost of (i) 1 book (ii) 299 books.

Solutions: (i) £4760 ÷ 598 = £7.96 (nearest penny)
(ii) *calculator display* × 299 = £2380.

NU3

Express 384 as the product of prime factors: hence express 1920 as the product of prime factors. A tree diagram can be used for the example question above. We start with a small prime, in this case $\boxed{2}$: $384 = \boxed{2} \times 192$.

$384 = 2^7 \times 3$; $1920 = 5 \times 384 = 2^7 \times 3 \times 5$.

NU4

$\dfrac{3+4}{2+5} = 1$; carelessness with a calculator could give 10.

In calculations of this type, where there are numbers above and below the line, one of the following methods should be used:

Method 1:
Calculate the part below the line and store it in $\boxed{\text{M+}}$; now input the part above the line, press $\boxed{=} \to \boxed{+} \to \boxed{\text{RM}} \to \boxed{=}$.

Method 2:
Input the part above the line, press $\boxed{=} \to \boxed{+} \to \boxed{(}$; now calculate the part below the line, press $\boxed{)}$ press $\boxed{=}$.

NU5
If $x = 50$ (to the nearest five), then $47.5 \leq x < 52.5$
If $x = 10$ (to the nearest whole number), then $9.5 \leq x < 10.5$

NU6
$2^3 = 8$; $\sqrt[3]{8} = 8^{1/3} = 2$.

NU7
$19000000 = 1.9 \times 10^7$ in standard index form (not 19×10^6)

$0.00034 = 3.4 \times 10^{-4}$. You should be familiar with the $\boxed{\text{SCI}}$ and $\boxed{\text{EXP}}$ buttons on your calculator.

NU8
$m = k^2 - n^2$; find m when $k = 8$ and $n = -8$.

Answer: $m = 8^2 - (-8)^2 = 0$. The answer $8^2 - - (8)^2$ is wrong.

NU9
'Given that $V = \frac{1}{3}\pi r^2 h$, find V when $r = 4$ and $h = 7$.'
Your calculator can handle this question without difficulty:
$\boxed{1}\ \boxed{\div}\ \boxed{3}\ \boxed{\times}\ \boxed{\pi}\ \boxed{\times}\ \boxed{4}\ \boxed{x^2}\ \boxed{\times}\ \boxed{7}\ \boxed{=}$ (giving 117 to 3 sig. figs.)

Important note: do not input estimates for $\frac{1}{3}$;
inputing $0.3 \times \pi \times 4 \dots$ is wrong.

NU10
Give a reasonable estimate for $\dfrac{6900 \times 1.01}{401 \times 0.26}$

Answer: $\dfrac{7000 \times 1}{400 \times \frac{1}{4}} = \dfrac{7000}{100} = 70$

Broadly speaking, in the question above, you should be able to work with the rounded figures in your head. The purpose of estimating is to ensure that your answer is of the right order; careless calculator work with the given example could have led to the wrong answer: 4.52 (3 sig. figs.)

NU11

A rational number can be expressed in the form $\frac{a}{b}$ where a and b are integers, for example $\frac{3}{8}$ is rational and so is 0.362 as $0.362 = \frac{362}{1,000}$.

An irrational number cannot be expressed as $\frac{a}{b}$ where a and b are integers. $\sqrt{2}$ and π are irrational.

All finite and repeating (recurring) decimals are rational. You should know the decimals for $\frac{1}{3}(0.\dot{3})$, $\frac{1}{6}(0.1\dot{6})$, $\frac{1}{9}(0.\dot{1})$.

Be wary of saying the root of something is irrational just because it looks complicated; for example $\sqrt{1\frac{24}{25}}$ is rational $\rightarrow$ $\sqrt{1\frac{24}{25}} = 1\frac{2}{5}$.

NU12

24,000 people (to 2 significant figures) attended a football match; the least possible number could have been 23,500, the greatest 24,499.

NU13

If $a = 10.8 \pm 0.5$ and $b = 12 \pm 0.5$, then;

the maximum value of ab

> = the maximum of a by the maximum of b
>
> = 11.3×12.5
>
> = 141.25

the minimum value of ab

> = the minimum of a by the minimum of b
>
> = 10.3×11.5
>
> = 118.45

$$= \frac{11.3}{11.5}$$

$$= 0.98 \text{ (2 sig. figs.)}$$

the minimum value of $\dfrac{a}{b}$ $= \dfrac{\text{the minimum of } a}{\text{the maximum of } b}$

$$= \frac{10.3}{12.5}$$

$$= 0.82 \text{ (2 sig. figs.)}$$

NU14

If $y = 10 \pm \frac{1}{2}$, then $100y$ ranges from 950 to 1,050;

the percentage error is $\dfrac{\frac{1}{2}}{10} \times 100 = 5\%$.

NU15

If $998 \leq x \leq 1,028$, we can write x in the form $a \pm b$. Find the mean of the limits: $\dfrac{998 + 1,028}{2} = 1,013$; each limit is 15 from this, giving $x = 1,013 \pm 15$.

Algebra

Formula: the quadratic equation $ax^2 + bx + c = 0$ has the solutions $x = \dfrac{-b \pm \sqrt{b^2 - 4ac}}{2a}$

AL1

When searching for the next term in a number pattern, it helps to look at the differences between the terms; if the first differences (d) are all the same, as above, the nth term is $\boxed{d \times n \pm \text{constant}}$. The constant is found by inspection ($4 \times n$ should generate the four-times table, but each term has to have 3 subtracted to match the given sequence).

AL2

In harder sequences you may have to go on to the second difference (or higher) to find the next term:

The encircled figures can be worked out by following the arrows; you should check that the next term is 56.

The nth term in this case is a quadratic expression, involving n^2. You may, in elementary cases, find the nth term by comparing the sequence to : 1, 4, 9, 16,...n^2; the nth term in the given sequence is $n^2 + n$.

AL3

$3^{15} \times 3^2 = 3^{17}$ and not 3^{30}.
When multiplying you add the indices.

$3^8 \div 3^2 = 3^6$.
When dividing you subtract the indices.

AL4

The reciprocal of $\frac{2}{3}$ is $\frac{3}{2}$; the reciprocal of 5 is $\frac{1}{5}$.

For a mixed number e.g. $3\frac{1}{2}$, first write it as a vulgar fraction: $3\frac{1}{2} = \frac{7}{2}$; then 'turn it upside down': $\frac{2}{7}$ is the reciprocal of $3\frac{1}{2}$.

You should familiarise yourself with the $\boxed{\frac{1}{x}}$ button on your calculator. The product of an expression and its reciprocal is 1.

AL5

(i) If $-6 < x \le 4$, this could be shown on the number line as:

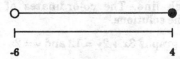

(ii) integer values of x satisfying the inequality are -5, -4, -3, -2, -1, 0, 1, 2, 3, 4.

AL6

If $x^4 = 46$, we can find x to any degree of accuracy by trial and improvement.

Try $x = 2$: $2^4 = 16$, so 2 is too small.
Try $x = 3$: $3^4 = 81$, so 3 is too large.

Now try the mean of the two: $\dfrac{2+3}{2} = 2.5$.

Try $x = 2.5$: $2.5^4 = 39$, so 2.5 is too small.

We now know that the root lies between 2.5 and 3, so try the mean of these two: $\dfrac{2.5+3}{2} = 2.75$.

Try $x = 2.75$: $2.75^4 = 57$, so 2.75 is too large.

We now know that the root lies between 2.5 and 2.75, so try the mean of these two: $\dfrac{2.5+2.75}{2} = 2.625$.

Try $x = 2.625$; the rest is left to the candidate.
($x = 2.6$ to 1 decimal place.)

AL7

Solve the equations $3x - 2y = 17$ and $2x - 3y = 13$.

The co-efficients of x are different, as are those of y; let us make the co-efficients of y equal:

Multiply $3x - 2y = 17$ by 3: $9x - 6y = 51$
Multiply $2x - 3y = 13$ by 2: $4x - 6y = 26$

Now subtract the two rows: the y's vanish, giving $5x = 25$; so $x = 5$. We can now find y by substitution: $3 \times 5 - 2y = 17$, giving $y = -1$.

Candidates sometimes get confused about whether to add or subtract the two rows; you only add when the signs are mixed

e.g. $\left.\begin{array}{l} +3m \\ -3m \end{array}\right\}$ otherwise you always subtract.

AL8

To solve simultaneous equations by graphical methods, draw the graph of each line. The co-ordinates of the point of intersection give the solutions.

Example: solve by graphs $3x + 2y = 12$ and $y = 2x - 1$.

To draw the graph of $3x + 2y = 12$, complete the table below;

x	0	?
y	?	0

$\rightarrow$

x	0	4
y	6	0

This method is useful when the letters are on the same side of the equals sign. Plot the points (0,6) and (4,0) and join them with a straight line.

To draw the graph of $y = 2x - 1$, complete the table below:

x	0	1	2
y	?	?	?

$\rightarrow$

x	0	1	2
y	-1	1	3

(You could have chosen a different set of x-values.)

Plot the points (0,-1), (1,1) and (2,3), and join them with a straight line. The diagram below shows the lines intersecting at (2,3); the solutions are: $x = 2$ and $y = 3$.

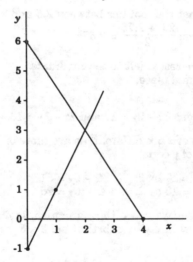

AL9

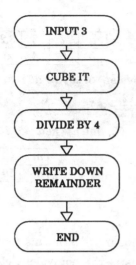

Here 27 ÷ 4 = 6 remainder 3, so 3 is written down; relying on a calculator could lead to a wrong answer in this case:

27÷ 4 = 6.75; 0.75 is *not* the remainder.

AL10

(i) $\sqrt[4]{x} = x^{1/4}$;

e.g. $\sqrt[4]{81} = 81^{1/4} = 3$ (verify with your calculator).

(ii) $\sqrt[4]{x^3} = x^{3/4}$

You can think of this as: cube x then find its 4th root, or find its 4th root first and cube the result. In numerical examples the second method is often the easier

e.g. $\sqrt[4]{81^3} = 81^{3/4} = 3^3 = 27$.

AL11

Direct Proportions:

(i) 'b varies as a', means $b = ka$, where k is a constant.

a	1	2	3
b	5	10	15

In this table $b = 5a$.

(ii) 'b varies as the square of a', means $b = ka^2$, where k is a constant.

We can find a relationship between a and b if we know two values.

Example: If $b = 100$ when $a = 5$, then $b = ka^2$;
substituting $a = 5$ and $b = 100$, we get $100 = k \times 25$, giving $k = 4$.

The relationship between a and b is $b = 4a^2$.

Inverse Proportions:

(i) '*b* varies inversely as *a*' means that $b = \dfrac{k}{a}$, where k is a constant, this is the equivalent of saying $ab = k$.

a	2	3	3.2	12
b	6	4	*m*	1

In the table $ab = 12$, so $m = \dfrac{12}{3.2} = 3.75$

Example: If $m = 40$, when $n = 50$, find n when $m = 25$.

Answer: mn is constant;
$40 \times 50 = 2000$
$25 \times ? = 2000$

m	40	25
n	50	?

This gives $? = \dfrac{2000}{25} = 80$.

(ii) '*b* varies inversely as the square of *a*' means that $b = \dfrac{k}{a^2}$ where k is a constant; this is the equivalent of saying $a^2b = k$. We can find a relationship between a and b if we know two values.

Example: If $b = 32$ when $a = \frac{1}{4}$, then $a^2b = k$; substituting $a = \frac{1}{4}$ and $b = 32$ we get $\left(\frac{1}{4}\right)^2 \times 32 = k$. Simplifying we get $k = 2$.

The relationship is $a^2b = 2$.

AL12
Factorise: $3x^2y - 6x^3y^2$.

Examine each part for common factors: 3 is a common factor, so is x^2, so is y. Hence we get $3x^2y(1 - 2xy)$; don't slip up by putting zero before the minus sign! If in doubt expand your answer.

AL13

This graph refers to the cost of a job. Let the graph run until it cuts the vertical axis. This intercept (£15) is the basic fee (call-out charge). The gradient of the line $\left(\dfrac{10}{1} = 10\right)$ gives the rate in £'s per hour; the equation of this line is

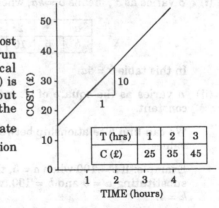

T (hrs)	1	2	3
C (£)	25	35	45

$$C = 10T + 15$$
$$\uparrow \qquad \uparrow$$
gradient   basic charge

AL14

(a) Rearrange the formula $m = c + at$ to make a the subject:

step 1: $m - c = at$; step 2: $\dfrac{m - c}{t} = a$; so $a = \dfrac{m - c}{t}$

(b) Rearrange the formula $k = \frac{1}{2}x^2y$ to make x the subject:

step 1: $2k = x^2y$; step 2: $\dfrac{2k}{y} = x^2$, so $x = \sqrt{\dfrac{2k}{y}}$.

AL15

Expand $(3x + 4)(5x - 9)$; you can think of this as a rectangle with its area to be calculated:

	$3x$	$+4$
$5x$	$15x^2$	$+20x$
-9	$-27x$	-36

the 'area' of each section is written in the appropriate box; the total 'area' is $15x^2 - 7x - 36$.

Hence $(3x + 4)(5x - 9) = 15x^2 - 7x - 36$.

Some books use the method below, where the arrows show multiplication:

$(3x + 4)(5x - 9)$ giving $15x^2 - 27x + 20x - 36$.
The result is the same as above.

AL16

Solve (i) $2x + 3 < 17$; cancel off 3, to get $2x < 14$, so $x < 7$.

Solve (ii) $x^2 \leq 25$; careful! $\sqrt{25} = \pm5$, so $-5 \leq x \leq 5$. If in doubt test some values on both sides of 5, and of -5.

Solve (iii) $x^2 \geq 100$; $\sqrt{100} = \pm10$ so $x \geq 10$ or $x \leq -10$.

Solve (iv) $29 \geq 4x + 1 \geq 17$; take one part at a time:
$29 \geq 4x + 1$ so $x \geq 7$
$4x + 1 \geq 17$ so $x \geq 4$

Hence x is, 4, 5, 6, 7 (for integer solutions) or $4 \leq x \leq 7$ in general.

AL17

The graphs of quadratics look like this:

('cups' or 'caps')

The graphs of cubics look like this:

The graphs of reciprocals (e.g. $y = \frac{a}{x}$, $a < 0$)

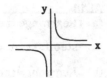

When talking about real-life graphs, pay particular attention to the details on the axes; the graph below, for example, shows the volume of water in a bath increasing while the water is flowing, then a period where it is constant while the bath is being taken, and finally the emptying of the bath.

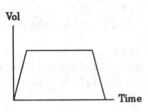

AL18

a	1	2	3	4
b	3	12	27	48

If $b = ka^n$, we can find k and n by substitution.

Substituting $a = 1$ and $b = 3$, we get $3 = k \times 1^n$, so $k = 3$.
Substituting $a = 2$ and $b = 12$, we get $12 = 3 \times 2^n$, so $n = 2$.

Hence the relationship is $b = 3a^2$.

AL19

$x^{-2} = \frac{1}{x^2}$ and $\frac{1}{x^3} = x^{-3}$; $x^0 = 1(x \neq 0)$

$y^{2/3} \times y^{-1/2} = y^{2/3-1/2} = y^{1/6}$. (See also AL3)

AL20

To solve equations by graphical methods, draw the graphs of the expressions and see where they intersect.

Suppose you have drawn the graph of $y = x^3 - 3$ and you are asked to use it to solve the equation $2x^3 + x - 6 = 0$. Rewrite the new equation to be solved in terms of the original expression:

$$2x^3 + x - 6 = 0 \Rightarrow 2x^3 - 6 = -x \Rightarrow x^3 - 3 = \frac{-x}{2}$$

You must now draw the graph of $y = \frac{-x}{2}$ and see where it intersects the first g   ph.

AL21

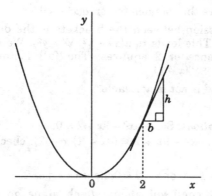

To find the gradient at the point $x = 2$, draw a tangent at the point where $x = 2$; make a convenient triangle; read the h and b values from *the axes*, not from your ruler. The gradient is $\frac{h}{b}$.

The gradient gives the rate of change at the point of tangency: in distance/time graphs this is the velocity at that instant; in velocity/time graphs it gives the acceleration.

AL22

If $x_{n+1} = \sqrt{x_n + 20}$, and $x_1 = 4.8$,

then $x_2 = \sqrt{4.8 + 20} = \sqrt{24.8} \approx 4.97$ (do not clear your calculator)

then $x_3 = \sqrt{4.97... + 20} \approx 5$.

The sequence of values is convergent; 5 is the limit. If there is no clear limit a sequence is divergent.

We can find the limits by letting: $x_{n+1} = x_n = x$.

For the formula above we get $x = \sqrt{x + 20}$, giving $x^2 = x + 20$.

Rearranging we get $x^2 - x - 20 = 0$.

This quadratic has solutions 5 and -4.

By rewriting the quadratic $x^2 - x - 20 = 0$, as $x(x - 1) = 20$, we get another iteration formula: $x_{n+1} = \dfrac{20}{x_n - 1}$

Try $x = -3.8$, and see what happens. Your sequence of numbers should converge to -4, which is the second root of the quadratic above.

AL23
(i) Factorise $x^2 - 16$; this is the difference of 2 squares:
$x^2 - 16 = (x + 4)(x - 4)$.

(ii) Factorise fully $ax^4 - ay^4$.

First remove the common factor: $a(x^4 - y^4)$

The expression between the brackets is the difference of 2 squares. This leads to $a(x^2 + y^2)(x^2 - y^2)$. We again have the difference of 2 squares. The full factorisation is $a(x^2 + y^2)(x + y)(x - y)$.

Note: $x^2 + y^2$ is not factorisable.

AL24

Quadratic Equations: Solve $4x^2 - 9x + 2 = 0$.

(a) *By factors*: $4x^2 - 9x + 2 = (4x - 1)(x - 2)$; check by using AL15.

Either $4x - 1 = 0$ or $x - 2 = 0$, hence $x = \frac{1}{4}$ or 2.

If you get confused about which signs go inside the brackets, note that +2 in the expression above is the product of either $(+2) \times (+1)$ or $(-2) \times (-1)$.

(b) *By completion of the square*: make the coefficient of x^2 equal to 1;

$4x^2 - 9x + 2 = 0$

$4x^2 - 9x = -2$

$x^2 - \frac{9}{4}x = \frac{-1}{2}$ (Dividing through by 4)

$x^2 - \frac{9}{4}x + \left(\frac{-9}{8}\right)^2 = \frac{-1}{2} + \left(\frac{-9}{8}\right)^2$;

$\left(\frac{-9}{8} \text{ is } half \text{ of } \frac{-9}{4}; \text{ its square is added to both sides} \right)$

$\left(x - \frac{9}{8}\right)^2 = \frac{49}{64}$; hence $x - \frac{9}{8} = \pm \frac{7}{8}$.

$x - \frac{9}{8} = + \frac{7}{8}$ or $x - \frac{9}{8} = -\frac{7}{8}$,

giving $x = \frac{7}{8} + \frac{9}{8} = 2$ or $\frac{-7}{8} + \frac{9}{8} = \frac{1}{4}$

(c) *By the formula* (given at the start of this section)

$4x^2 - 9x + 2 = 0$, so $a = 4$, $b = -9$ and $c = 2$.

$x = \dfrac{9 \pm \sqrt{49}}{8}$

$x = \dfrac{9 + 7}{8}$ or $\dfrac{9 - 7}{8}$, giving $x = 2$ or $\frac{1}{4}$

Note: all quadratic equations can be solved by the formula - if you are having trouble factorising, use the formula (unless you are told otherwise).

If the quadratic is written 'back-to-front' e.g. $3 + 2x - x^2 = 0$, then $a = -1$, $b = 2$ and $c = 3$.

AL25

Simplify: $\dfrac{1}{x + 7} + \dfrac{2}{x + 8}$

$$\frac{1}{x + 7} + \frac{2}{x + 8} = \frac{1(x + 8) + 2(x + 7)}{(x + 7)(x + 8)} = \frac{3x + 22}{x^2 + 15x + 56}$$

AL26

Express $4x^2 - 2x + 29$ in the form $(ax + b)^2 + c$, where $a > 0$.

Expanding the second expression we get $a^2x^2 + 2abx + b^2 + c$. We now match this off term-for-term with the original:

$a^2 = 4$, $2ab = -20$, and $b^2 + c = 29$. Hence $a = 2$, $b = -5$ and $c = 4$.

Therefore $4x^2 - 20x + 29 = (2x - 5)^2 + 4$.

One advantage of writing the expression like this is that we can tell the minimum value of the function: as $(2x - 5)^2 \geq 0$ for all values of x, the whole expression has a minimum of 4, when $x = 2\frac{1}{2}$.

AL27

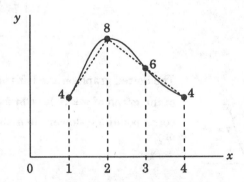

To estimate the area under a curve divide it into trapezia. The area under this curve is:

$$\text{Area} = \tfrac{1}{2}(4 + 8) \times 1 + \tfrac{1}{2}(8 + 6) \times 1 + \tfrac{1}{2}(6 + 4) \times 1$$

$$= 6 + 7 + 5$$

$$= 18 \text{ sq. units.}$$

In velocity/time graphs the area tells us how far something has travelled.

AL28
Graphs from Graphs

This is a sketch of the graph of $y = x^2$.

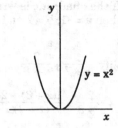

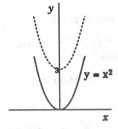

The dotted graph on the left is a sketch of the graph $y = x^2 + 3$. It is a translation three units along the y-axis in the positive direction.

The dotted graph on the right is a sketch of the graph of $y = 3x^2$. It is 'narrower' and correspondingly higher than the graph of $y = x^2$.

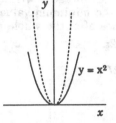

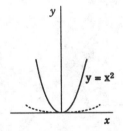

The dotted graph on the left is a sketch of the graph of $y = \frac{x^2}{3}$. It is 'broader' and correspondingly lower than the graph of $y = x^2$.

The graph of $y = \frac{1}{x^2}$ on the right does not exist when $x = 0$. For very small values of x, y is very large, for very large values of x, y is very small. The dotted graph is a sketch of $y = \frac{1}{x^2}$.

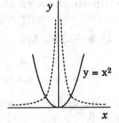

Shape and Space

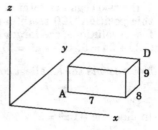

SS1

If a cuboid measuring $7 \times 8 \times 9$ is placed on the axes such that A is on the origin and the edges just touch the three axes, then the co-ordinates of D are (7, 8, 9).

SS2

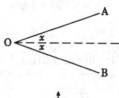

The points which are equidistant from OA and OB lie on the bisector of the angle $A\hat{O}B$.

SS3

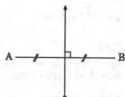

The locus of points which are equidistant from A and B lie on the perpendicular bisector of AB.

Note: the word 'perpendicular' is essential, as you could have an oblique bisector.

SS4

In three dimensions, the locus of a point which moves such that it is a fixed distance from a given point is a sphere.

The locus of a point which moves such that it is equidistant from two parallel planes is a plane half way between the two and parallel to them.

SS5

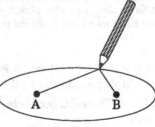

If two points, A and B, are fixed and a taut piece of string is fastened to them, the pencil point will trace an ellipse.

SS6

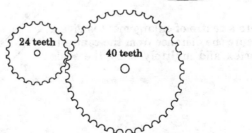

24 teeth

40 teeth

If the two cogs are rotated from this position they will return to
this position '120 teeth' later. The smaller cog will have made
five revolutions, the larger one three revolutions.
(120 ÷ 24 = 5, 120 ÷ 40 = 3)

Note: 120 is the smallest common multiple of 24 and 40.

SS7
In diagram (i), $x^2 = 5^2 + 12^2 = 169$,
so $x = \sqrt{169} = 13$cm.

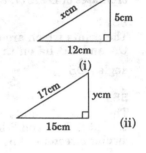

(i)

In diagram (ii), $17^2 = y^2 + 15^2$,
so $y^2 = 17^2 - 15^2 = 64$

$y = \sqrt{64} = 8$cm.

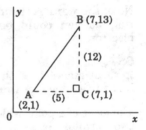

(ii)

SS8
The distance between A and B is
found by using Pythagoras:

$AB^2 = 5^2 + 12^2 = 169$.

So AB = 13 units.

SS9
Before carrying out calculations in plane and solid shapes, check
the formulas you are about to use from the formula sheet. A
trapezium need not have its parallel sides horizontal!

SS10
To enlarge the rectangle by scale factor
$1\frac{1}{2}$, multiply its sides by $1\frac{1}{2}$; $6 \times 1\frac{1}{2} = 9$ and
$4 \times 1\frac{1}{2} = 6$. The enlarged rectangle is 9cm
by 6cm.

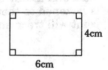

Where a centre of enlargement is given,
measure the distance from the centre to
a vertex and multiply it by the scale
factor.

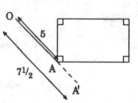

64

For example, to enlarge the rectangle by scale factor $1\frac{1}{2}$, centre
O, multiply OA (5 units) by $1\frac{1}{2}$, this gives $7\frac{1}{2}$ which means the
image of A is $7\frac{1}{2}$ units from O along the line OA. You now do the
same for the other vertices.

SS11

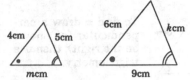

Find the length of the sides marked k and m.

The triangles are similar so we can think of the bigger one as an
enlargement of the smaller one; the scale factor is
$6 \div 4 = 1\frac{1}{2}$

Hence $k = 1\frac{1}{2} \times 5 = 7\frac{1}{2}$cm and $m = 9 \div 1\frac{1}{2} = 6$cm.

SS12
On a map town A is 5cm from town B; the scale is 1:600000.
Calculate how far A is from B in kilometres.

The distance is $\dfrac{5 \times 600000}{100 \times 1000} = 30$km.

(100cm = 1m, 1000m = 1km)

SS13
In trigonometric problems, use the relevant formulas which can
be found at the back of this book. A few examples are given
below:

(i) Find y:
OPP = HYP × Sin of angle
(from formula sheet)

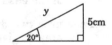

$5 = y \times$ Sin 20°, giving $y = 5 \div$ Sin 20°.

$y = 14.6$cm (3 significant figures)

(ii) Find q
OPP = ADJ × Tan of angle
(from formula sheet)

$5 = 10 \times$ Tan $q°$,
giving Tan $q° = 5 \div 10 = 0.5$.

$q° = $ Tan^{-1} 0.5 = 26.6° (3 significant figures)

SS14

In harder measurement problems always try to work in right-angled triangles. This will often mean having to draw in perpendicular lines.

Example

To find $\hat{x}$ draw a perpendicular (as shown on the right); then use trigonometry.

Example

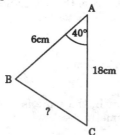

Here we can find BC by creating right-angled triangles (as shown on the right). Find x, y and z. Then use Pythagoras.

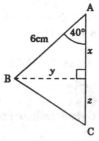

SS15

The three expressions $2\pi r$, $2\pi rh$, and $\pi r^2 h$ refer to different aspects of the cylinder.

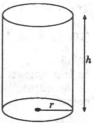

$2\pi r$ uses only one variable once (r), which suggests a single dimension and hence length. It is the circumference of the base of the cylinder.

$2\pi rh$ uses two dimensions multiplied ($r \times h$), which suggests area. It gives the area of the curved surface.

$\pi r^2 h$ uses three dimensions ($r \times r \times h$), which suggests volume. It gives the volume of the cylinder.

SS16

(a) If $\mathbf{a} = \begin{pmatrix} 2 \\ 9 \end{pmatrix}$ and $\mathbf{b} = \begin{pmatrix} 3 \\ -4 \end{pmatrix}$ then $2\mathbf{a} + 3\mathbf{b} = \begin{pmatrix} 4 \\ 18 \end{pmatrix} + \begin{pmatrix} 9 \\ -12 \end{pmatrix} = \begin{pmatrix} 13 \\ 6 \end{pmatrix}$

(b) If $\mathbf{a} = \begin{pmatrix} 3 \\ -1 \end{pmatrix}$ and P = (4,3), the image, P', of P after a translation of $2\mathbf{a}$ is $(4 + 6, 3 - 2) = (10,1)$. P' = (10,1).

(c) ABCD is a square;

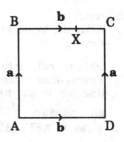

$\vec{AB} = \vec{DC} = \mathbf{a}$; $\vec{AD} = \vec{BC} = \mathbf{b}$.
Although the sides of the square
are equal, we can only give parallel
sides the same vector expressions.

If X divides BC in the ratio 3:1,
$BX = \frac{3}{4}\mathbf{b}$ and $XC = \frac{1}{4}\mathbf{b}$

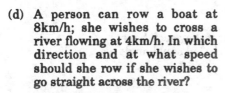

$$\vec{AX} = \vec{AB} + \vec{BX} = \mathbf{a} + \tfrac{3}{4}\mathbf{b};$$

$$\vec{DX} = \vec{DC} + \vec{CX} = \mathbf{a} - \tfrac{1}{4}\mathbf{b}$$

(d) A person can row a boat at
8km/h; she wishes to cross a
river flowing at 4km/h. In which
direction and at what speed
should she row if she wishes to
go straight across the river?

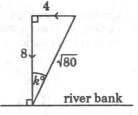

She should row at $(90 - k)°$ to
the bank.

$\hat{k} = \text{Tan}^{-1} \frac{4}{8} = 26.6°$. She should row at 63.4° to the bank at
8.9km/h.

(e) On an object a force of 8N acts due
East and a force of 6N acts due
South; what single force will balance
them?

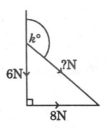

Use Pythagoras to find the force and
Trigonometry to find the direction.

ANS: 10N at 127°.

SS17

In three dimensional problems involving calculations of lengths and angles
always try to work in triangles.

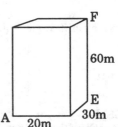

Example:

The tank shown measures 20m × 30m
× 60m.

Calculate
(i) the length of the diagonal AF;
(ii) the angle the diagonal makes with the base.

Solution:
(i) AF is the hypotenuse of a triangle as shown;

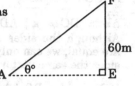

we can calculate it by using Pythagoras twice. The dotted line AE is the base diagonal, and measures $\sqrt{1300}$ by Pythagoras; so $AF^2 = \left(1300\right)^2 + 60^2 = 4900$; $AF = 70m$.

(ii) the angle which the diagonal makes with the base is the angle $\theta°$; it is found by trigonometry: $\theta° = \text{Sin}^{-1}\frac{60}{70} = 59.0°$.

SS18
Congruent Triangles
Two triangles are congruent if they each have:
(i) 2 equal sides and an included equal angle e.g.

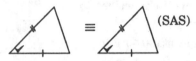

or
(ii) all sides equal e.g.

or
(iii) 2 angles equal and a corresponding side e.g.

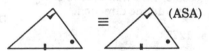

or
(iv) a right angle, equal hypotenuse, and an equal side e.g.

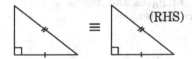

SS19
(a) **Similar Objects:**
If two solids are *similar*, the surface area of one multiplied by the scale factor *squared* gives the surface area of the other.

68

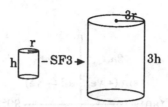

The volume of one, multiplied by the scale factor *cubed*, gives the volume of the other.

	SMALL	LARGE
sur. area	30cm²	270cm²
vol.	60cm³	1620cm³

Example: for the two similar cylinders the scale factor is 3; hence the surface area of the larger one is 3^2 times that of the smaller one. (30cm² × 9 = 270cm²)

The volume of the larger one is 3^3 times that of the smaller one. (60cm³ × 27 = 1,620cm³)

(b) When finding areas and volumes, substitute into the appropriate formula from the back of the book. You will find advice on this in NU9.

SS20

The length of the arc shown is:
$2 \times \pi \times 40 \times \dfrac{70}{360} = 48.9cm.$
The area of the sector is:
$\pi \times 40^2 \times \dfrac{70}{360} = 977cm^2$, which is

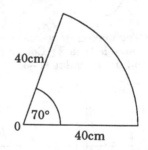

$\dfrac{7}{36}$ of the area of the circle from which it was cut.

SS21

$\text{Sin A}\hat{\text{B}}\text{D} = \text{Sin A}\hat{\text{B}}\text{C}$
$\text{Cos A}\hat{\text{B}}\text{D} = -\text{Cos A}\hat{\text{B}}\text{C}$
$\text{Tan A}\hat{\text{B}}\text{D} = -\text{Tan A}\hat{\text{B}}\text{C}$

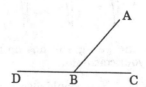

SS22

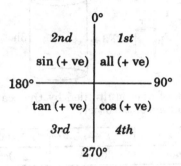

The diagram shows which trigonometric ratios are positive (+ve) in each quadrant, e.g. Cos 290° is positive as 290° is in the 4th quadrant; its Tan and Sin are negative.

SS23
Trigonometric Graphs
Sin x and Cos x:

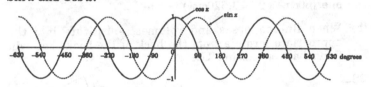

The maximum value of Sin x is 1, the minimum value is –1; the same is true for Cos x. The maximum value of 3 Sin x is 3, the minimum value is –3.

Tan x:

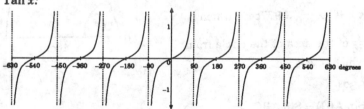

Note: the Tan graph has no maximum value – try Tan 89.9° with your calculator.

Important: You should also consult AL28 'Graphs from graphs'.

SS24
Circle Theorems

(i)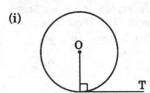

the angle between the radius and tangent is 90°.

(ii)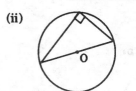

the angle in a semicircle is 90°.

(iii)

the angle at the centre of a circle is twice the angle at the circumference.

(iv)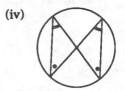

angles in the same segment are equal.

(v)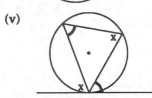

the angle between a tangent and a chord is equal to the angle in the alternate segment.

(vi)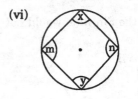

the opposite angles of a cyclic quadrilateral add up to 180°; $\hat{x} + \hat{y} = \hat{m} + \hat{n} = 180°$.

(vii)

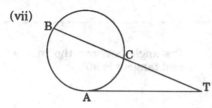

If TA is a tangent, TA² = TB.TC.
Example: If TB = 25cm, and TC = 16cm, then
TA = $\sqrt{25 \times 16}$ = 20cm.

SS25

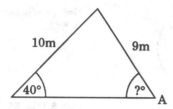

To find $\hat{A}$ use the *Sin Rule*; note the triangle is not right-angled, and we are dealing with 2 sides and 2 angles:

$$\frac{10}{\text{Sin A}} = \frac{9}{\text{Sin } 40°}; \text{ so Sin A} = \frac{10 \text{ Sin } 40°}{9}$$

giving $\hat{A}$ = 45.6°.

SS26

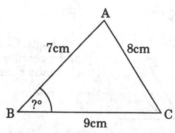

To calculate $\hat{B}$ we use the *Cosine Rule*; the Sin Rule would not help as we are not using 2 angles:

$$8^2 = 7^2 + 9^2 - 2 \times 7 \times 9 \text{ Cos B}$$
$$64 = 49 + 81 - 126 \text{ Cos B}$$
$$64 = 130 - 126 \text{ Cos B}$$
$$-66 = -126 \text{ Cos B}$$

(It would be very wrong to write 64 = 4 Cos B.)

So Cos B = $\frac{66}{126}$; $\hat{B}$ = 58.4°.

SS27

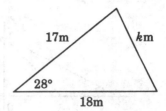

To find k we use the *Cosine Rule*:

$k^2 = 17^2 + 18^2 - 2 \times 17 \times 18 \cos 28°$

$k = 8.52$m (3 significant figures).

SS28
Combinations of transformations
(i)   A translation followed by a translation is a translation.

(ii) A reflection followed by a reflection is a rotation. If the axes of reflection are perpendicular, the object makes a half-turn about the point of intersection.

(iii) An enlargement followed by an enlargement is an enlargement.

(iv) A reflection followed by a rotation (or vice versa) is a reflection.

SS29
Inverse Transformations
(i)   The inverse of an enlargement scale factor k is an enlargement scale factor $\frac{1}{k}$.

(ii) The inverse of a reflection in a mirror line is a reflection in the same mirror line.

(iii) The inverse of a translation $\begin{pmatrix} a \\ b \end{pmatrix}$ is a translation $\begin{pmatrix} -a \\ -b \end{pmatrix}$

(iv) The inverse of a rotation of $k°$, is a rotation of $360 - k°$, about the same centre.

SS30
Matrices and Transformations
When you are asked to find what transformation a given matrix corresponds to, e.g. $\begin{pmatrix} -1 & 0 \\ 0 & 1 \end{pmatrix}$ you can draw a little diagram and apply the matrix to it.

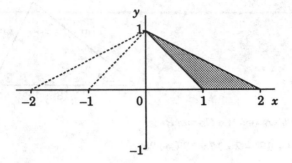

Applying the matrix to the shaded triangle we get

$$\begin{pmatrix} -1 & 0 \\ 0 & 1 \end{pmatrix}\begin{pmatrix} 0 & 1 & 2 \\ 1 & 0 & 0 \end{pmatrix} = \begin{pmatrix} 0 & -1 & -2 \\ 1 & 0 & 0 \end{pmatrix}$$

Plotting the new co-ordinates, we see the transformation is a reflection in the y-axis.

If you are asked to find a matrix corresponding to a given trans-formation, e.g. a rotation of 90° about (0,0), the following method is helpful:

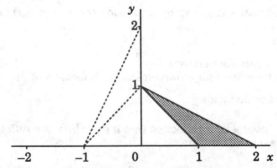

Draw a shape and its image under a 90° rotation about (0,0).

Set up matrices as follows for the shape and its image:

$$\begin{pmatrix} & \\ & \end{pmatrix}\begin{pmatrix} 0 & 1 & 2 \\ 1 & 0 & 0 \end{pmatrix} = \begin{pmatrix} -1 & 0 & 0 \\ 0 & 1 & 2 \end{pmatrix}$$

Now the blank matrix which represents the transformation can be filled in by inspection to give

$$\begin{pmatrix} 0 & -1 \\ 1 & 0 \end{pmatrix}$$

Handling Data

Formula: s.d $= \sqrt{\dfrac{\Sigma(x - \bar{x})^2}{n}}$ or $\sqrt{\dfrac{\Sigma x^2}{n} - \left(\dfrac{\Sigma x}{n}\right)^2}$

HD1
Questionnaires: There are broad guidelines for drawing up a questionnaire; these include politeness to interviewees, a guarantee of anonymity, unbiased questions (not, for example, 'what do you think of that ugly supermarket?'). Questions should be easily answered – frequently a tick box is the best method for this.

Keep your hypotheses simple, 'politically minded people tend to live in suburbs' would be a very tricky hypothesis to test because some of the words in it are hard to define.

HD2
Finding the mean from grouped data:

MARKS	MID-POINT	FREQUENCY
0-9		1
10-19		4
20-29		9
30-39		5

First find the mid-point values: 4.5, 14.5, 24.5, 34.5.

The mean is: $\dfrac{1 \times 4.5 + 4 \times 14.5 + 9 \times 24.5 + 5 \times 34.5}{1 + 4 + 9 + 5} = 24.0$

This is only an estimate of the mean as we do not know how the marks are distributed within the groups.

HD3
In the above distribution the modal group is 20-29 (not 9!).
The median is the middle value of the 19 data, so it is the 10th and is in the group 20-29.

HD4
The range is the difference between the largest and the smallest values:
Set A: 2, 3, 4, 2, 4, 3, 4, 3   Set B: 8, 10, 9, 9, 9, 8, 10.
The range of each set is 2. (In A: 4 – 2 = 2, B: 10 – 8 = 2.)

HD5
A frequency polygon
is formed by joining
the midpoints of the
tops of the bars of a
histogram.

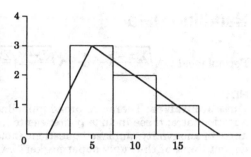

HD6
When interpreting a flow diagram it helps to keep a table as
shown:

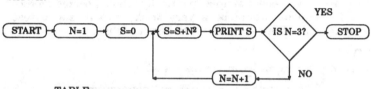

TABLE

N	PRINT
1	1
2	5
3	14

HD7
When drawing a line-of-best-
fit, try to get the same numbers of values on either side
of the line; a transparent
ruler helps!

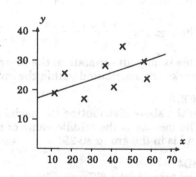

HD8

Shoe Size	4	5	6	7	8
Frequency	2	5	8	9	1

The probability of a child chosen from this group having a size 6
foot is $\frac{8}{25}$. In a similar group of 150 we could reasonably expect $\frac{8}{25}$
of 150, i.e. 48 pupils to have size 6.

HD9

When you toss a die you cannot get a two and a three in one throw – these events are *mutually exclusive*; the probability of getting either a two or three in one throw is: $\frac{1}{6} + \frac{1}{6} = \frac{2}{6} = \frac{1}{3}$.

HD10

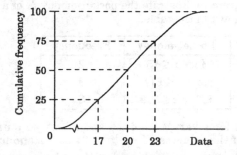

The graph shows a cumulative frequency. We can find the median and the quartiles as follows:

the median is the middle value of the total frequency, so dot across from 50 and read off the data axis to get 20.

The lower quartile is the 25th value, which is 17.
The upper quartile is the 75th value, which is 23.
The *interquartile range* is $23 - 17 = 6$ (not $75 - 25 = 50$!)

HD11

If a die is thrown twice, what are the chances that 5 comes up each time?

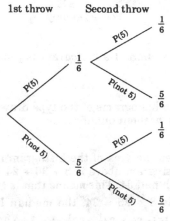

The tree diagram shows what could happen; the answer is $\frac{1}{6} \times \frac{1}{6} = \frac{1}{36}$. The outcomes of the second throw are independent of those for the first throw.

HD12

Draw a histogram to illustrate the pocket-money £x of a group of children as shown in the table.

Pocket-money	Frequency
£1 < x ≤ £5	2
£5 < x ≤ £11	9
£11 < x ≤ £19	6

The intervals for x vary, i.e. £4, £6 and £8, so we must adjust the heights of the columns. If we take £4 as a standard width, then £6 is $1\frac{1}{2}$ widths, so the height of the column representing £5 < x ≤ £11 is $9 \div 1\frac{1}{2}$ which is 6. £8 is two widths, so the column representing £11 < x £19 is $6 \div 2$, which is 3. The histogram can now be drawn.

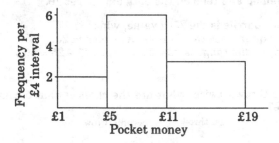

HD13

The area of each column of a histogram is proportional to the frequency.

HD14

The vertical axis in histograms of the type drawn should not be labelled 'frequency' without qualification.

HD15

The median divides the area of the histogram into two halves; the area of the histogram above is 8 + 36 + 24 = 68, hence the median makes each half 34. This means that is goes through the middle column. As 8 + 26 = 34, the median lies $\frac{26}{36} \times 6 = 4\frac{1}{3}$ along the column. It is £5 + £$4\frac{1}{3}$ = £$9\frac{1}{3}$, about £9.33.

HD16
Sampling
(a) A random sample is one in which every member of the population has an equal chance of being selected. It is frequently carried out by giving every member a number, and then making a random selection from those numbers using a calculator or computer.

(b) A stratified sample is one in which the population is divided into strata and members are randomly chosen from each stratum. The number of members chosen from each stratum is proportionate to its size.

(c) A quota sample is one in which the size of the sample is decided on, and categories of interest to the sampler are given a quota. For example, to sample 100 people's views on a new shampoo, the sampler might ask 40 people in the age range 15-25 yrs, 30 people in the age range 26-40 yrs, and 30 over 40's to answer a questionnaire.

(d) A systematic sample is one in which a starting point is chosen at random and members are then selected according to a pattern. For example, a customs officer stops a person at random, and then stops every 20th person after that.

(e) A cluster sample is one in which the population is divided into a number of small sections which are in themselves clusters of smaller groups. Then some of these smaller groups are randomly selected to make up the overall sample. For example, to sample the growth of seeds in a field a farmer might first decide to divide it into, say 8 sections, and then take a random square metre of seeds from each section. All the seeds together would constitute the sample.

HD17
If 70% of boys and 40% of girls sampled in a college go to church, this suggests that $\dfrac{70\% + 40\%}{2}$ = 55% of the children attend church. This conclusion is only valid if the number of boys is the same as the number of girls.

Consider a school with 40 girls and 160 boys, with the same sample results as above, now:

$$\frac{0.7 \times 160 + 0.4 \times 40}{200} = 64\%.$$

This suggests that 64% of the children attend church.

HD18

A bag contains 4 Red and 5 Green marbles. Draw a tree diagram to illustrate what could happen if two marbles are drawn out without replacement.

The probabilities for the second draw are conditional on what happens in the first draw (compare HD11).

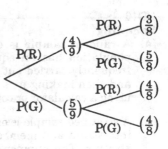

HD19

Find the standard deviation of 1, 2, 3, 4, 5, 6, 7, 8, 9, 10.

The mean is 5.5. We now use on of the formulas in the introduction:

$$\text{s.d} = \sqrt{\frac{(1-5.5)^2 + (2-5.5)^2 + (3-5.5)^2 \dots + (10-5.5)^2}{10}}$$

$$= 2.87 \text{ (3 sf)}$$

OR

$$\text{s.d} = \sqrt{\frac{1^2 + 2^2 + 3^2 \dots + 10^2}{10} - (5.5)^2}$$

$$= 2.87 \text{ (3 sf)}$$

Important: You could use the $\boxed{\text{STAT}}$ facility on your calculator to work out the standard deviation but, while this is very convenient, it is also very dangerous! If you make a slip in feeding in the figures, the examiner will have nothing by which to judge your work, so you may score zero. It is much better to use one of the methods set out above so that the examiner can see your working, and then verify the result with a calculator.

HD20

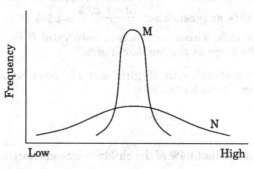

Distribution M has a much smaller range of values than distribution N; N has more high values.

HD21
The normal dis-
tribution curve is
symmetrical about
the mean, and bell-
shaped.

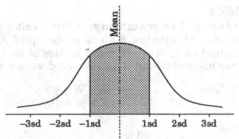

The shaded area taken up by one s.d. on either side of the mean
is a little over 68% of the distribution. If we shaded two s.d. on
either side we would have 95%, while three s.d. on either side
gives 99.7% i.e. practically the whole distribution.

Note: A curve which is bell-shaped need not refer to a normal
distribution; you should check it against the criteria above.

HD22
In this diagram, the
completion time is
16min (not 15) and
the slack time is
1min (16 − 15).

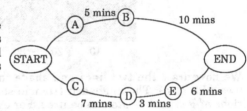

HD23

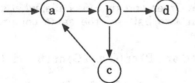

A network should
not have a loop.

HD24

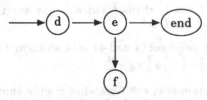

A network should not have a dangling item; f is going nowhere.

HD25

Linear Programming: A wine seller can have at most 40 bottles of wine on a shelf made up of Red and White; there should be at least 10 more bottles of Red than of White. Make two inequalities in R and W and draw a diagram.

Solution:
$$R + W \leq 40$$
$$R \geq W + 10.$$

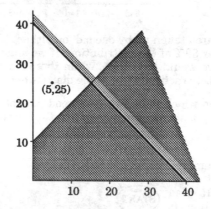

We now draw the two lines and shade the unwanted regions (see AL8 also). The unshaded triangle shows which combinations of Red and White can be used. For example five bottles of White and 25 of Red satisfy the conditions.

HD26

A bag has four Red, five Green and six Blue balls; what are the chances of picking out two balls of the same colour if no replacement takes place?

Solution: We could get (R and R) or (G and G) or (B and B), that is:

$$\frac{4}{15} \times \frac{3}{14} + \frac{5}{15} \times \frac{4}{14} + \frac{6}{15} \times \frac{5}{14} = \frac{62}{210} = \frac{31}{105}.$$

HD27

If a six-sided die is thrown twice, what are the chances of getting *at least* one four?

Solution: We could get (4 and 4) or (4 and non-4) or (non-4 and 4), that is $\frac{1}{6} \times \frac{1}{6} + \frac{1}{6} \times \frac{5}{6} + \frac{5}{6} \times \frac{1}{6} = \frac{11}{36}$.

A neater solution is to ask first what are the chances of getting (non-4 and non-4), that is $\frac{5}{6} \times \frac{5}{6} = \frac{25}{36}$. The remaining $\frac{11}{36}$ is for at least one four.

Section 3 – Answers to the one-hour practice papers

In this section you will find all the answers to the questions in Section 1 and a marking scheme to enable you to record and interpret your marks for each paper.

You can record your marks in the table below.

Paper	Marks
1	
2	
3	
4	
5	
6	
7	
8	
9	
10	
11	
12	
13	
14	
15	

Paper One

1 (a) $179.5 \le d < 180.5$m [2]

   (b) $179.25 \le d < 179.75$m [3]

   (c) £707.07 [2]

   (d) CAN $ 1.36 [3]

2 (a) $\begin{pmatrix} 14 \\ -15 \end{pmatrix}$ [2]

   (b) 4 [3]

   (c) 3 [2]

   (d) (7,-16) [3]

3 (a) 4 [1]

   (b) 2.10×10^{-5} [3]

   (c) 2×10^7 [4]

   (d) multiplied by 10 [2]

4 (a) Sampling in which every member of the population has an equal chance of being selected. [2]

   (b) (i) You must know which category each member of the population is in.

      (ii) You need to know the size of each category.

      (iii) If members from one (or more) category under-respond, it could be difficult to draw worthwhile conclusions.

     Take full credit for any two of the above points [2]

   (c) Choose randomly from each form, as shown. [3]

Year	Y7	Y8	Y9	Y10	Y11	L6	U6
No. of pupils	12	12	12	12	12	6	6

   (d) Make allowances for boys and girls being fairly represented in the numbers selected in (c). [3]

5 (a) List 1 $\begin{bmatrix} i \\ ii \end{bmatrix} \begin{bmatrix} ii \\ iii \end{bmatrix} \begin{bmatrix} iii \\ i \end{bmatrix}$
      List 2 [2]

Section 3

(c)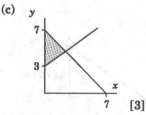

[3]

(d) $y > 0, x > 0, y < 2x + 3, x + y < 7$ [2]

4 (a) 16.6° [2½]

(b) 3.54cm [2½]

(c) 82cm [2½]

(d) $\dfrac{\text{Area of old}}{\text{Area of new}} = \dfrac{1^2}{\left(\sqrt[3]{2}\right)^2} \approx 63\%$ [2½]

5 (a) (ii) & (iii) [2]

(b) e.g. $\sqrt{2} \times \sqrt{2} = 2$ [2]

(c) $\sqrt{180} = \sqrt{36}\sqrt{5} = 6\sqrt{5}$ [3]

(d) $\sqrt{162} = 9\sqrt{2}$ [3]

6 (a) 2.73 [3]

(b) Her English marks are more consistent than her Maths marks. [1]

(c) $\dfrac{102}{325}$ [3]

(d) $\dfrac{23}{144}$ [3]

[Total 60 marks]

Paper 3

1 (a) 8.86cm^2 [3]

(b) 13.7m^2 [3]

(c) 63.75m^2 [2]

(d) 956.25m^3 [2]

2 (a) 13.8cm [2]

(b) Yes; the scale factor is 0.75 $\left(\dfrac{4.5}{6} = \dfrac{7.5}{10} = 0.75 \right)$ [3]

(c) 200km [3]

(d) 17.5cm [2]

3 (a) **32** [3]

(b) 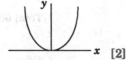 [2]

(c) $ab = 24$ [3]

(d) 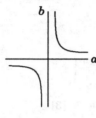 [2]

4 (a) $7\pm\frac{1}{2}$ [2]

(b) **99** [3]

(c) $\frac{2}{3}$ [2]

(d) $\frac{1}{10} + \frac{2}{30} = \frac{1}{6}$ [3]

5 (a) **15** [3]

(b) **19, 4,000** [2]

(c)

[4]

(d) **Frequency** [1]

6 (a) $\pi(R + r)(R - r)$ [$2\frac{1}{2}$]

(b) **10cm** [$2\frac{1}{2}$]

Section 3

(c) $x(x + 8) = 75$ ∴ $x^2 + 8x + 16 = 91$ etc. [$2\frac{1}{2}$]

(d) 5.54 [$2\frac{1}{2}$]

[Total **60** marks]

Paper 4

1 (a) $2^2 \times 5^2 \times 17$ [3]

(b) $2^2 \times 5^3 \times 17$ [2]

(c) $1,200 + 70 + 5$ [2]

(d) e.g. $\boxed{23}\boxed{+}\boxed{76}\boxed{\times}\boxed{48}\boxed{=}\boxed{+}\boxed{(}\boxed{(}\boxed{86}\boxed{+}\boxed{24}\boxed{)}\boxed{=}$
for a scientific calculator. [3]

2 (a) (i) = Volume (ii) = Area (iii) = Perimeter [3]

(b) $\binom{14}{1}$ [2]

(c) 3m [2]

(d) 56.3° [3]

3 (a)

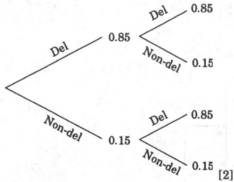

[2]

(b) 0.7225 [3]

(c) 0.0225 [2]

(d) 0.255 [3]

4 (a) 70% [1]

(b) 76% [3]

(c) (i) it gives information about each category or stratum of the population.

(ii) we can deduce results about the whole population.

(iii) it is representative of the population. [3]

(d) (i) may not be representative of the population.

88

(ii) it can be time-consuming to administer.

(iii) non-response could lead to bias. [3]

5 (a) $q \neq kp$, where k is a constant. [2]

(b) $a = \frac{1}{2}, n = 2$ [3]

(c) 7 [2]

(d) $\frac{7}{16}$ [3]

6 (a) $n^2 + n - 30 = 0$ [2]

(b) 5, –6 [3]

(c) $\dfrac{1}{n+3} + \dfrac{1}{n+4} = \dfrac{2n+7}{(n+3)(n+4)}$ [3]

(d) 1 [2]

[Total 60 marks]

Paper 5

1 (a)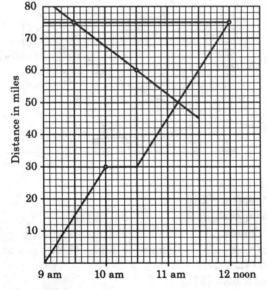

[3]

(b) 11.10am [3]

(c) -4, -3, -2, -1, 0, 1, 2 [2]

(d) -4, -3, -2. [2]

2 (a) £14000 [3]

(b) £19250 [3]

   (c) £16750 [2]
   (d) £5250 [2]
3 (a) 53.1 [2]

   (b) $\dfrac{1.2}{\text{Cos }53.1} = 2$ [3]

   (c) 0.96km [3]
   (d) 143° [2]

4 (a) $\pi, \sqrt{2}+1$ [2]

   (b) 1 [2]
   (c) 1 [3]

   (d) $\dfrac{5\sqrt{3}+3\sqrt{3}}{2\sqrt{3}} = 4$ [3]

5 (a) 2, 2,8, 4, 5.7, 8 [2]

   (b)

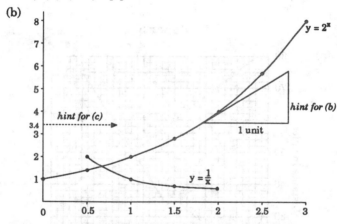

   2.4 [3]
   (c) 1.8 (approx.) [2]
   (d) 0.65 (approx.) [3]

6 (a) 25 minutes [3]
   (b) all of tasks *a*, *b* and *c* must be finished before any one of *d*, *e*, *f* can begin. [3]
   (c) it has a loop. [2]
   (d) G is dangling. [2]

[Total 60 marks]

Paper 6

1 (a) 26 [2]
   (b) 240 [3]
   (c) 59/120 [3]
   (d) A fair spinner would give about 24 for each number, so the chances of an even number are 48/120. [2]

2 (a) 4.2×10^6 [2]
   (b) 2.6×10^4 [3]
   (c) 1.2×10^{-3} [2]
   (d) 2.5×10^{-15} [3]

3 (a) 8.55km [3]
   (b) 23.5km [2]
   (c) 81.4° [3]
   (d) 23.7km [2]

4 (a) 20m/s [3]
   (b) -20m/s [2]
   (c) 4m/s^{-2} [2]
   (d) 28s [3]

5 (a) 3, 6, 7, 9 [2]
   (b) $\frac{1}{16}$ [3]
   (c) 5.299: express this to 3 significant figures or to 2 places of decimals. (Note to candidate: there are different answers.) [2]
   (d) 1.7m [3]

6 (a) 63 [4]
   (b) It has travelled 63m [1]
   (c)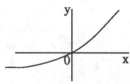
   [2]
   (d)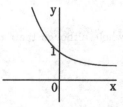
   [3]

[Total 60 marks]

Paper 7

1 (a) 21.875lbs [2]
   (b) 452kg [3]
   (c) 68.58cm [2]
   (d) 167 feet [3]
2 (a) (i) & (iii) [2]
   (b) 1m [2]
   (c) 43.8° [2]
   (d) 20.5cm [4]
3 (a) HHH, HHT, HTH, HTT, THH, THT, TTH, TTT [3]
   (b) $\frac{4}{8} = \frac{1}{2}$ [2]
   (c)

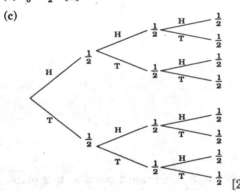

[2]

   (d) $\left(\frac{1}{2}\right)^3 \times 4 = \frac{1}{2}$ [3]

4 (a) 36π [2]
   (b) 2cm [3]
   (c) 13N [2]
   (d) 113° [3]
5 (a) 4 [2]
   (b) $3^x \times 5 \times 10^6$ [3]
   (c) $3^{-2} \times 5 \times 10^6$ [2]
   (d) about 14 weeks old. [3]
6 (a) Y8 has better kickers on the whole although their range is wider. [2]
   (b) 5 [2]
   (c) 68% [2]
   (d) (i) 48 [2] (ii) 60 [2]

[Total 60 marks]

Paper 8

1 (a) 5, 15, 3 respectively [3]

   (b) It rotates anti-clockwise at a rate of 150. [2]

   (c) B turns anti-clockwise, C and D turn clockwise. [2]

   (d) B and D (anti), C (clock) [3]

2 (a) The question is too blunt: try "tick the appropriate box for the size of your family":

Children	0	1	2	3	4	more
Number						

[2½]

   (b) the words 'religious' and 'larger' are difficult to define. [2½]

   (c) People have more time to consider their replies. [2½]

   (d) People may not bother responding. [2½]

3 (a) 2^7 [2]

   (b) 5 [2]

   (c) £6475 [3]

   (d) 3.4375 [3]

4 (a) $\hat{G} = \hat{E} = 90°$; AG = CE = 5cm; GF = EF = 3cm(SAS) [4]

   (b) $\dfrac{5}{\sqrt{34}}$ [2]

   (c) $\dfrac{-3}{\sqrt{34}}$ [2]

   (d) $\dfrac{-5}{3}$ [2]

5 (a) $\dfrac{25}{102}$ [3]

   (b)

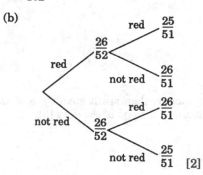

[2]

(c) $\frac{1}{2}$ [3]

(d) $\frac{25}{51}$ [2]

6 (a) 6.56, 6.81, 6.92 [2]

(b) converging [1]

(c) $r^2 - 6r - 7 = 0, r = 7$ or -1 [4]

(d) $x^2 - 6x - 7 = 0, x(x - 6) = 7 \therefore x = \dfrac{7}{x - 6}$ [3]

[Total 60 marks]

Paper 9

1 (a) 0 [1]

(b) 0,1 [3]

(c) $5I + 7H = 290$ and $I + H = 50$ [3]

(d) 20 Higher books [3]

2 (a) 10, 30, 60, 85, 100 [2]

(b)

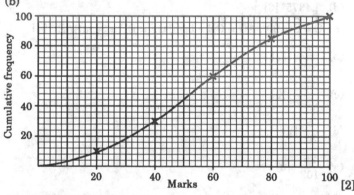

[2]

(c) (i) 56 (ii) 36 [4]

(d) 76 [2]

3 (a) $y^{1/3}$ [1]

(b) $\sqrt{m^3}$ or $\left(\sqrt{m}\right)^3$ [3]

(c) He started with some money, then spent steadily, and was left with a smaller amount at the end of the day. [3]

(d) $h = \dfrac{3V}{\pi r^2}$ [3]

4 (a) $-6, 1, 8.6$ [1]

(b)

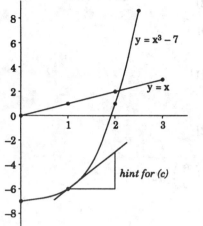

$y = x^3 - 7$

$y = x$

hint for (c)

[3]

(c) 3 [3]

(d) $y = x^3 - 7$; $y + 7 = x^3$; $\dfrac{y+7}{x^3} = 1$; $x^{-3}(y+7) = 1$ [3]

5 (a) 5.63cm [3]
  (b) 1.88cm [3]
  (c) 70.5° [2]
  (d) 1:8 [2]
6 (a) 41.0° [2]
  (b) 3m [3]
  (c) 145m [2½]
  (d) 87.3° [2½]

[Total 60 marks]

Paper 10

1 (a) $4n - 1$ [2]
  (b) $n^2 - 1$ [2]
  (c) 336 and 504 [3]
  (d) $n(n - 1)(n + 1)$ or $n^3 - n$ [3]
2 (a) 1.8×10^8 [3]
  (b) 2×10^{-5}s [3]
  (c) 2×10^{12} [2]
  (d) 3.125×10^{-4} [2]

3 (a) $7x(x - 8y)$ [3]

   (b) $r = \sqrt{\dfrac{V}{\pi h}}$ [3]

   (c) 5.51 [3]

   (d) $81x^2 - 225$ [1]

4 (a) 18.9cm [3]

   (b) 69.9° [3]

   (c) 1,000cm³ [2]

   (d) 1,600 [2]

5 (a) $\begin{pmatrix} 6 \\ -4 \end{pmatrix}$ and $\begin{pmatrix} 6 \\ 8 \end{pmatrix}$ [2]

   (b) $\begin{pmatrix} 3 \\ 4 \end{pmatrix}$ [2]

   (c) WX is parallel to OB, and half its length. [3]

   (d) Hint: Show that ZY is parallel to OB and half its length. [3]

6 (a) $A + B \le 1{,}700$ [2]

   (b) $10A + 15B \ge 1{,}800$, so $2A + 3B \ge 3{,}600$ [3]

   (c)

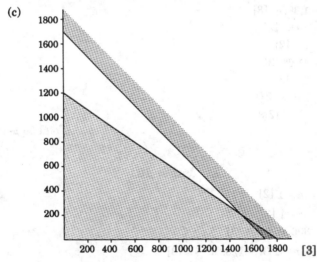

[3]

   (d) 1,500m² of A and 200m² of B. [2]

[Total 60 marks]

Paper 11

1 (a) 2.7,

Try	Too big	Too small
2.5		✔
2.75	✔	
2.625		✔
2.6875	✔	
2.65625		✔

The last 2 'tries' are each 2.7 to 1 decimal place. [3]

(b) 25 [2]

(c) 1, -1 [2]

(d)

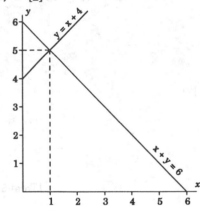

$x = 1, y = 5$ [3]

2 (a) 20cm [1]

(b) 60cm² [3]

(c) $-44\frac{1}{2}$ [3]

(d) 0.805 or $\frac{103}{128}$ [3]

3 (a) 64 [3]

(b) 20 [3]

(c)
```
 -3                    4
 ●────────────────────○
```
[2]

(d) (8,4), (9,3), (10,2), (11,1), (12,0). [2]

4 (a) If the school operates a policy of mixed-ability forms. [2]

(b) If the school streams its intake on the basis of reading tests. [2]

(c) If there are equal numbers of boys and girls. [2]

(d) 10 boys, 190 girls. [4]

5 (a) 36.9°, 143.1° [2]

(b)

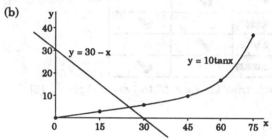

; 25.3° [3]

(c) $\left(\dfrac{\sqrt{3}}{2}+1\right)\mathbf{b}$ [3]

(d) $\dfrac{\mathbf{a}}{2}+\left(\dfrac{\sqrt{3}}{2}+1\right)\mathbf{b}$ [2]

6 (a) 0.5 [2]

(b) 0.84 [3]

(c) 2.44 ± 0.81 [3]

(d) 0.9% [2]

[Total 60 marks]

Paper 12

1 (a) 3, 4, 4, 6, 2 [2]

(b) 145.5cm [3]

(c) 54 [3]

(d) The question allows the answer, 'I do not know' which is not useful. The group could have asked each child to tick a box appropriate to his or her height e.g.

120-129☐, 130-139✔, 140-149☐, 150-159☐, 160-169☐.
[2]

2 (a) a = (iii) [$2\frac{1}{2}$]

(b) b = (ii) [$2\frac{1}{2}$]

(c) c = (i) [$2\frac{1}{2}$]

(d) d = (iv) [$2\frac{1}{2}$]

3 (a) angles same: 40, 60, 80 [2]

  (b) $x = 2.25$cm, 8cm [3]

  (c) 5.0cm [2]

  (d) $\dfrac{12}{\text{Cos}\,22.6°} = 13.0$cm [3]

4 (a)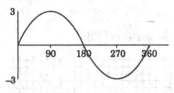

  [2]

  (b)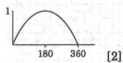

  [2]

  (c)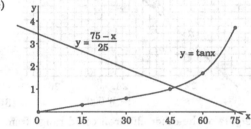

  [2]

  (d) Draw $y = \dfrac{75-x}{25}$; $x \approx 47$ [4]

5 (a) $26.6°, 206.6°$ [3]

  (b) $330°$ [2]

  (c) 3cm^2 [3]

  (d)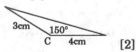

  [2]

6 (a) $\dfrac{x+3}{x+2}$ [2]

  (b) $(2x-5)^2 + 17$ [3]

  (c) $x(x+2) = 210$ [2]

  (d) 13.53mm [3]

[Total 60 marks]

Paper 13

1 (a)

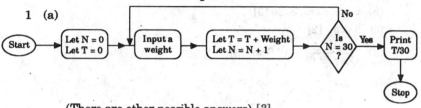

(There are other possible answers) [3]

(b)/
(c)

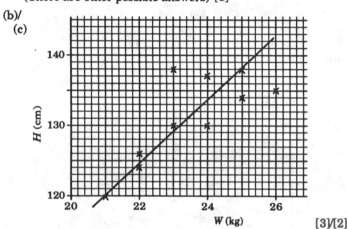

[3]/[2]

(d) No; the weights of the other children could range from, say, 30kg to 35kg or 60kg to 65kg. [2]

2 (a) Translation: $\begin{pmatrix} 7 \\ 0 \end{pmatrix}$ [3]

(b) (9,5) [2]

(c) Translation: $\begin{pmatrix} -1 \\ -3 \end{pmatrix}$ [3]

(d)

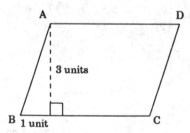

$\hat{B} = \text{Tan}^{-1}\frac{3}{1} = 71.6°$ (3 sig. figs.) [2]

3 (a) Volume [2]
  (b) Surface Area [3]
  (c) Perimeter [$2\frac{1}{2}$]
  (d) diagonal of base or top. [$2\frac{1}{2}$]
4 (a) 20, 25, 24, 24 [3]
  (b) Frequency [1]
  (c) $\frac{1}{2}$ the area [2]
  (d) £5,760 if values are equally distributed. [4]
5 (a) $k + \frac{3}{4} = 1; k = \frac{1}{4}$ [2]
  (b) $2^{-6} \times 2^{4y} = 2^3; y = 2\frac{1}{4}$ [3]
  (c) 1.07 [2]
  (d) £$P(1.07)^n$. [3]
6 (a) Rotation of 90° (anti-clockwise) about (0,0) [3]
  (b) Reflection in $y = x$ [3]
  (c) Enlargement, by scale factor 2, centre (0,0) [2]
  (d) Reflection in $y = -x$ followed by (c) or vice versa.[2]

[Total 60 marks]

Paper 14

1 (a) 4.5, 14.5, 24.5, 34.5, 44.5 [1]
  (b) 28.5 [3]
  (c)

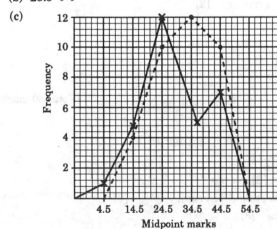

Midpoint marks [3]

   (d) The new graph should be higher on the right hand side, as shown by the dotted lines. [3]

2 (a) 3^6 [2]

   (b) $3\frac{5}{8}$m [4]

   (c) $(0.8)^3 < 1$, so answer must be less than 27. [3]

   (d) She divided: $27 + (0.8)^3$ [1]

3 (a)

        0   [3]

   (b) 12 [2]

   (c) 16 [2]

   (d) $-6 \le y \le 6$; -6, -5 ... +5, +6. [3]

4 (a) 3 [3]

   (b) 3 [2]

   (c) (i) $\to b$ [2]

   (d) (ii) $\to a$ [3]

5 (a) 49.7cm [3]

   (b) 216° [3]

   (c) 9:4 (or equivalent) [2]

   (d) 27:8 (or equivalent) [2]

6 (a) 30° [2]

   (b) 15° [3]

   (c) $67\frac{1}{2}$° [2]

   (d) 7cm [3]

[Total 60 marks]

Paper 15

1 (a) (6, 3, 2) [2]

   (b) 6.3 units [3]

   (c) Plane bisecting FE at right angles. [2]

   (d) 13.4 units^2 [3]

2 (a) $2\frac{1}{2}$ [3]

(b) $4x(x + 2y)$ [2]

(c) $x = \sqrt{\dfrac{v-n}{m}}$ [2]

(d) ± 10 [3]

3 (a) $20000 \times \frac{1}{2} = 10000$ [2]

(b) $\dfrac{18000}{60} = 300$ [3]

(c) Yes: $\dfrac{70 \times 0.8}{20} = \frac{56}{20}$; $\frac{40}{20} = 2$, $\frac{60}{20} = 3$,

so $\frac{56}{20}$ is between 2 and 3. [2]

(d) No; $\dfrac{750 \times 4}{100} = \dfrac{3000}{100} = 30.$ [3]

4 (a)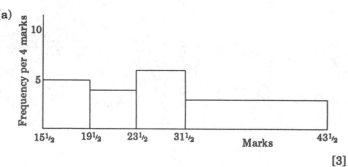

[3]

(b) 13 [3]

(c) 24-31 [1]

(d) $4\frac{1}{5}$ [3]

5 (a) $a + b$ [2]

(b) $\frac{1}{2}b - \frac{1}{6}a$ [3]

(c) 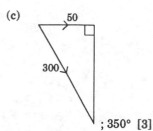 ; 350° [3]

(d) 296mph [2]

103

6 (a) $\begin{pmatrix} 1 & 0 \\ 0 & -1 \end{pmatrix}$ [3]

 (b) $\begin{pmatrix} \frac{1}{2} & 0 \\ 0 & \frac{1}{2} \end{pmatrix}$ [2]

 (c) $\begin{pmatrix} 0 & -1 \\ 1 & 0 \end{pmatrix}$ [3]

 (d) $\begin{pmatrix} 0 & 1 \\ 1 & 0 \end{pmatrix}$ [2]

[Total 60 marks]